REFLECTIONS
OF GOD'S TURNING
POINTS

A Personal Testimony

NANETTE H. KIRK

WESTBOW
P R E S S®
A DIVISION OF THOMAS NELSON
& ZONDERVAN

Scripture taken from the King James Version of the Bible.

Scripture quotations marked NLT are taken from the Holy Bible, New Living Translation, copyright 1996, 2004, 2007. Used by permission of Tyndale House Publishers, Inc. Carol Stream, Illinois 60188. All rights reserved.

Scripture quotations marked NKJV are taken from the New King James Version. Copyright 1982 by Thomas Nelson, Inc. Used by permission. All rights reserved.

WestBow Press books may be ordered through booksellers or by contacting:

WestBow Press
A Division of Thomas Nelson & Zondervan
1663 Liberty Drive
Bloomington, IN 47403
www.westbowpress.com
1 (866) 928-1240

ISBN: 978-1-9736-0930-8 (sc)
ISBN: 978-1-9736-0932-2 (hc)
ISBN: 978-1-9736-0931-5 (e)

Library of Congress Control Number: 2017917996

Print information available on the last page.

WestBow Press rev. date: 1/12/2018

I dedicate this book to God Almighty, who allowed some things to happen in my life to give testimony of His unfailing love and to come to know His truth. God is my Savior, my strength, and deliverer. As I reflect upon how far I have come, I am reminded of 2 Samuel 22:1–4. It is a favorite hymn written by David, a king after God's own heart. It was the day the Lord delivered him from the hand of all his enemies and delivered him from the hands of Saul, the king of Israel that was appointed by God. Saul was so overcome with jealousy of David that he allowed his jealousy to lead him to the decision to kill David. David spoke the following words to the Lord:

> **The Lord is my rock, my fortress, and my deliverer; the God of my rock in Him will I trust: he is my shield, and the horn of my salvation, my high tower, and my refuge, my savior; thou savest me from violence. I will call on the Lord, who is worthy to be praised: so shall I be saved from mine enemies. When the waves of death compassed me, the floods of ungodly men made me afraid; the sorrows of hell compassed me about; the snares of death prevented me; in my distress I called upon the Lord, and cried to my God: and he did hear my voice out of his temple, and my cry did enter his ears. 2 Samuel 22:1-4 (KJV)**

I feel the same way David did when the Lord delivered me from often difficult or critical situations that could have led to my demise but instead led to turning points in my life. Above all, He has been faithful to His promise to never leave me or forsake me.

I give thanks to God for loving me unconditionally. I give thanks to Jesus for His obedience and His blood and to the Holy Spirit, who led me to the truth. I give much thanks to my now deceased mother. Although dealing with her own demons, she had the wherewithal to cover me with her prayers as I walked in ignorance and worldliness. I rode on the wings of her prayers for years, not realizing that she was on her knees for me and my siblings even though she was homeless.

I give thanks to my husband, Jim, for being a man of God. He has also loved me with an unconditional love, allowing and encouraging me to be all that God has called me to be. His wisdom, self-sacrifice, understanding ways, and peace have contributed greatly to the success of this marriage. You are my best friend, and I am so committed to you and to our love, which we both agree was a match made in heaven.

I give thanks to my daughter, who gave me my first lesson in love by merely being born. I consider you my gift from God, a living testament to His wisdom. My love for you runs deeper than any river. Thanks for becoming a true woman of God. I give thanks to my son-in-law Lee for being a loving family man, and for allowing God to use you.

Thanks to my grandchildren for just being who you are and loving me. MeMom's love for you is endless.

Finally, I give thanks to all the people God used to get me to this place in life for such a time as this. You may or may not know who you are, but God knows, and when reflecting on my past, so do I.

This book is designed to reach people, especially women, both in the church and those living outside of God's will. It is for people who find themselves in what appear to be hopeless situations because they have made some poor decisions. I am a living witness for the most high God, and I write this book of testimony to encourage you and offer you hope through Jesus Christ, our Lord and Savior. I challenge you to trust in Him. My testimony is not unique—we all have them—and I don't expect my testimony to reach everyone. But God has called me to tell it, so it will reach the people He has ordained it to reach. You may or may not know who you are. It is my hope that in reading this testimony detailing what God has brought me through, you will realize that you need to know Him for yourself. There is nothing impossible with God.

I was working on a ministry project for my bachelor of science in urban ministry leadership. It was for our final grade. The focus of my ministry project was domestic violence. I had lived it, and I understood it. Part of the ministry project required us to write a narrative about our walk with the Lord. They wanted us to share how we came to know the Lord for ourselves and how we came to know our calling into the ministry. As I started reflecting back on all those years, I started thinking about how God's divine interventions saved my life many times. I reflected on all the uncertainty and instability in my prior life along with all the abuse, emotional pain, rejection, confusion, and violence that the Lord had brought me through triumphantly. I thought about the layers of emotional and psychological scarring it left upon my heart and how God in Jesus Christ has been working to peel back the layers to reveal the person He called me to be. As I reflect on the various turning points in my life, I can see where my entire life from childhood through adulthood has been in preparation for God's calling. I have lived a life of testimonies to the Lord, and everything that has affected my life has been a lesson for ministry. I call them turning points because with every poor decision made from living a sinful lifestyle filled with drama, abuse, volatile situations, and a lot of pain and suffering, God's divine interventions made that situation work for my good and for His glory. Each time I messed up, I had to rethink that situation and make a decision about whether I was going to stay in it or move out of it. Sometimes it was easy, and sometimes I had to learn the hard way. But once I made the decision to let go of a situation or people, I never looked back and never regretted making that decision. Hence, the *turning points.*

Between the ages of thirteen to thirty-nine, I was a saved woman walking in the way of the world. I was saved at the age of thirteen, but I did not know the Lord and had no real personal relationship with Him. Although not knowing Him and not walking in His will or living according to the standards set forth in His Word, God forgave me of my sins and proceeded to lead me into the path of righteousness. I received the gift of grace and mercy through Jesus Christ, my personal Savior, and God held fast to His promise to never leave me or forsake me. I have never regretted calling upon the Lord in the midnight of my mess. I know without a doubt that God exists and that He is real. He delivered me in a supernatural way that I will never forget, and I know that I am alive today to give testimony of His divine intervention into a situation that almost killed me. You will learn about my experience in this book. My hope is that you will know God through Jesus Christ for yourself. Some people think they have to clean up their acts before they come to Christ, but God will meet you right where you are. You don't have the power except through that which comes from above to turn your situation around.

If you are in a situation that seems hopeless, God will turn it around for your good and for God's glory in Jesus's name. Jesus came to give hope to the hopeless. God will meet you right where you are, using the amount of knowledge you have. **Luke 19:10** tells us that Jesus came to save that which was lost. I was one of the lost people until God saved me and delivered me. In Christ, we can find forgiveness, and that forgiveness changes our lives and our eternities. Jesus came to reconcile us back to God. There is no one else anywhere at any time who can qualify for that position. Praise to His almighty name!

Now with that being said, let me properly introduce myself. My name is Nanette Kirk, born Hilda Nanette Montgomery. I am a child of God, saved by His grace through the blood of Jesus Christ. I am a wife, mother, grandmother, nurse, and witness for the Most High. Why is this important to you? It's important because that was not the legacy written for me by my family. Their legacy was that I was born with *bad blood*, that I was never going to amount to anything, and that no man would ever want me. That was the mantra I heard almost daily from the mouth of my grandmother, with whom I lived for a portion of my life. I was reminded constantly of how I came from nothing and how I would amount to nothing. Are those words familiar to you? It all started in childhood. I was devalued. My self-esteem was eroded away, and the roots of that dictated the course of my early childhood into adulthood.

As I pondered this introduction, I asked God to tell me who I should say I am and how this testimony could influence those reading it in such a way that I was not the focal point. I want to make sure God gets the glory. *How, God, can this testimony get through the very core of what the people may see as a hopeless situation, and how can it plant that seed of hope that will lift up a heavy heart and manifest by Your grace as the root of a new beginning?* God wants you to know that you don't have to live a defeated life beset with generational curses. Just because someone tells you that you will never amount to anything doesn't mean you have to live out that lie. My biggest shame was that I was living a defeated life as a saved person. I have come to find out that just being saved is not enough. You must have a personal and committed relationship with God through our Lord and Savior, Jesus Christ, to have any victory in life. God is faithful to do what He said. I am a living witness of His promise. **"I will seek what was lost and bring back what was driven away, bind up the broken and strengthen what was sick" (Ezekiel 34:16 NKJV).**

I am sharing my testimonies to show the divine power of a living God and how He took a lost, lonely, sad, depressed, confused, and sinful wretch with low self-esteem like me, pulled me from the depths of my living hell, and brought godly change into my life. I want to tell of God's unmerited grace and the mercy He bestowed upon me when I humbled myself, fell prostrate before Him, and called upon His name in the midst of my darkness. I am reminded of this each time I read **2 Chronicles 7:14–16 (NKJV).**

> **Then if My people who are called by My name would humble themselves, and pray and seek My face, and turn from their wicked ways, then I will hear from heaven and will forgive their sin and heal their land. Now My eyes will be open and My ears attentive to prayer made in this place. For now I have chosen and sanctified this**

**house, that My name may be there forever; and
My eyes and My heart will be there perpetually.**

The first reflection that came to mind was my childhood. Why? Because that is where it all started. That's where the seeds of development are planted. I can still vividly see my grandmother planting the seeds of self-doubt and low self-esteem. I can hear her almost daily mantra of how my sister and I were never going to amount to anything. I feel her sharp, cutting words tearing down my self-confidence brick by brick as she predicts the expected shame we would bring upon the family. I often wondered, especially when I came to a point in my life where self-esteem played a large role, if my grandmother had any idea about the effect her words would have on me and on my life. In **James 3**, we are reminded that **"blessings and cursing come pouring out of the mouth."** The Word of God says that life and death are in the power of the tongue. The entire third chapter of the book of James teaches us about controlling the tongue. You can speak life into a person or situation, or you can speak death into it. My grandmother was a Christian, but even she had her faults and weaknesses. As a child I heard constant reminders of my parents' failures. I was made to feel guilty about those failures and carried the shame that accompanied the guilt as if it were my own, which made me dislike who I was. One thing I did not know was that God knew the path I would take in life from the time I was formed in my mother's womb. He knew that self-doubt, abuse, low self-esteem, and a long line of traumatic events were going to be the seeds He would use to prepare me for ministry. As I reflect, I see my early childhood environment as a training ground for what was to come. My early childhood conditioning was comparable to boot camp. A lot of the abuse and trauma I received in my life was delivered at the hands of the very people who were supposed to love me. It was a tough lesson in love with wounds so deep that only God could heal them. I believe that your early childhood experiences carve the templates from which you draw on during your life experiences. I have come to learn that if you don't know the Lord, you can run the gamut from one bad experience to another. I believe such seeds can easily manifest themselves as blossoms of self-destruction. As my self-esteem was eroding, I found myself in all sorts of unhealthy situations, and most led to some sort of abuse, be it physical, drugs, sexual, emotional, or mental confusion. Looking back now, I can see the blessing in the midst of all my despair. I still was better off than some. I am alive to tell it. Praise the Lord!

I am the daughter of an alcoholic father and a mentally ill mother. I never knew my biological father because he left when I was still a baby. My mother spent a lifetime in and out of the state mental hospital. She had been diagnosed as a paranoid schizophrenic. I am the second of six children, all of whom have a different father, except my older sister and me. We share the same father, although she got to know him, and I did not. I was born and raised in a suburban community in Pennsylvania. I had a very traumatic childhood, one that was loveless and filled with physical and emotional abuse. My parents were having problems in their marriage. We were living in Philadelphia at that time in the late 1940s and early 1950s. I was too young to pin it down to a definitive timeline. Some of what I do know from my birth to about three years old is what my mother told me before she died. My memory kicks in from about the age of four years and forward. My mother told me that when she and my father started having problems and were about to lose our home, she called my grandmother and asked if she could come home. She said Grandma (which is what my sister and I called her) told her she could come home, but my father could not come with her. It was no secret that my grandma did not like my father. She felt my mother married beneath her, and I am sure she did not like that my father was about thirteen or more years older than my mother. I've been told that my father went out to the store one day and never came back. I believe that started my mother on her own path of self-destruction.

After my parents separated, my mother started having a series of emotional breakdowns that resulted in her hospitalization. One time after having an argument with my grandmother, my mother decided she was moving and taking my sister and me with her. I remember the loud argument and how my grandmother tried to stop my mother from taking us out into the night. We were on the trolley car headed to Philadelphia, when Mom had another episode. She became paranoid and thought someone was following us. She had a breakdown, and the police came. Every time she would get out of the hospital, it would seem as if she was getting her life together, and then she would relapse. During this time it was just my older sister and me. My mom was hospitalized, and my sister and I were placed in a foster home. The separation from my parents and the rest of my family was the first turning point in my life. The blessing in it as I look back is that my sister and I were placed in the foster home together. Foster care was the beginning of a long line of different abuses. The foster family was physically and emotionally abusive. My sister and I spent a lot of time in the basement of that home. My sister was beat a lot. I was timid and afraid. I cried a lot. I was intimidated by all the verbal abuse, which was traumatic in itself. I was about four years old, and my sister was six. The abuse was so bad that every time someone would come down the steps to the basement, my sister and I would hide behind the washing machine and peer out, hoping that someone would not beat us. The foster family did not care about us. They had a bedroom fixed up and dressed with dolls for show. So when the caseworker came to visit, the family would show her the room where they said we were staying. However, after the caseworker left, the family closed the door was closed, and we never saw that room again. We actually slept in the basement. My sister says she still remembers the rats that crawled around down there. The abuse was exposed when my mother (during one of her functional periods) and my grandparents came to visit us in foster care. My mother told me that my grandfather took one look at us and told my grandmother to bring us home.

—✺—

My sister and I were moved from foster care and into my grandparents' home. This I see as the beginning of yet another turning point in my life. My grandparents were appointed guardians of me and my sister.

Now you would think going to live with grandparents was a good thing. My grandfather was a retired Baptist minister. My grandparents owned a lovely fifteen-room house in the suburbs, and they were well respected by the community. They owned some real estate and could well have been considered status symbols in our community. Little did my sister and I know what lay behind the doors to the big house. My grandmother had raised twelve of her thirteen children. One died early during childhood. My mother was the black sheep of my grandparents' twelve remaining children. My mother was labeled as rebellious, and she was determined to do her own thing. My grandmother was the matriarch and very controlling. There seemed to always be conflict between my mother and my grandmother. I'm sure my grandmother was disappointed with my mother. My mother was sixteen when she got pregnant with my sister, and my father was twenty-nine at the time. In those days when you got pregnant, there was a sense of shame that came with it. So either you got married, or you went down south to have the baby. My grandmother was always concerned about how things looked from the outside and what the church folk would think. So my parents got married. It would not last because although my father was a chef by profession, at that time he was working at the local YMCA. He drank a lot and never felt he measured up to my family. I'm sure that contributed to the problems my parents were having.

While my sister and I were in my grandparents' care, my mother gave birth to four more children. Each had a different father. It seemed that each time she got well and started a new life in a new relationship, it resulted in another pregnancy.

One of my younger sisters was adopted by my aunt. My other younger sister was taken by her father to live with him, and we never saw her again. My baby brother was born later during another one of my mother's functional periods. She did get a chance to raise him until he was about seven years old. Then she relapsed. I have two brothers, but I don't know the whereabouts of one.

—⁂—

Now you may be wondering why this is important to know. I want to show you where seeds were being planted. It was the beginning of doubt, a lack of self-worth, abandonment, and rejection. There are many people out there who have been raised under similar circumstances and can relate to how these situations make one feel. Many of you know the effect these experiences have had on your own lives.

I did not yet know how this early childhood experience would affect my life. One of the traumas that really hurt was the time when my sister was adopted by our aunt. My sister was now being raised as my cousin. We were never encouraged to bond. We never interacted when they came to visit. We acted like strangers in the same room. It was as if we were waiting for approval from someone so that we could speak to each other. It never came, and so it was that we never came to know each other until later in our adult lives.

My grandmother was the biggest influence in my life. Now

this was not a positive thing. She was the family matriarch, and it seemed that she was revered by other family members. To me at that stage of my life, my grandmother seemed larger than life. I was afraid of her. She was mean-spirited, and she could give you a tongue-lashing. She was moody and seemed unhappy even though she had acquired much and had become a successful business woman. She owned some properties, and she was the landlord to tenants who had great respect for her. She had a good business sense for someone with little education. She was married to my grandfather at the age of fourteen. My grandfather was seventeen. They married young in those days. One would think she would have more joy after all she had accomplished. But her unhappiness serves as proof that having nice things and being successful in life doesn't make you happy. Although a domestic by occupation, she learned much of her business sense from the professional people she worked for. Her employers liked her and had great respect for her. Her attitude was such because she was probably tired after raising twelve of her own children. And now she found herself raising grandchildren. She made it perfectly clear to me and my sister that she did not feel like raising any more children.

It was soon clear that our rescue from the foster home had nothing to do with love. As a matter of fact, I never received an expression of love from her. As a matter of fact, I was never told that I was loved by anyone in my family, not even my grandmother. I was an adult when I first heard the words "I love you," and the expression did not come from a family member.

My grandmother was very outspoken and did not hide her feelings. She would strongly stress how we were a burden to her. She was angry frequently with my sister and me. She was argumentative. As I look back, I now believe she had some mental issues of her own but that she was never diagnosed. Besides, who was going to confront the matriarch? A lot of the family depended on her. She was a go-getter and knew how to get things done. The anger she felt toward my mother was clearly directed at me and my sister. We were reminders of my mother's failures. My grandmother predicted that my sister and I would embarrass the family. She reminded us daily that our father was a "no good alcoholic" and "our mother was crazy." This mantra was accompanied by reminders of how we were "born of bad blood," and then she cursed us by saying, "You are never going to amount to anything." She would compound it by saying, "No man will ever want you." For many years into adulthood, I believed that lie.

I learned heavy responsibility at an early age. Domesticity was the focal point of my upbringing. By the age of nine years old, I was proficient in cooking and cleaning. My grandparents never pushed education with us. She felt it was important that we know how to clean and cook. Her expectations of us were low because she truly felt we were not going to amount to anything, so she would teach us the basics of a domestic education. She knew that well because she cleaned houses for a living. My grandfather worked at the local mill and pastored a Baptist church. My grandparents married very young. She was fourteen, and Granddad was seventeen years old. I'm sure that marrying at such an early age and having twelve babies back to back had a lot to do with the way my grandmother felt by the time my sister and I were brought into their lives.

By the age of ten, my sister and I were cooking large meals to accommodate the family and church folk who would often come for Sunday dinners. Most of the people we served were family members who were married. My grandmother had great respect for them. She seemed to enjoy letting my sister and I know which cousins were going to college, even though she did not push education for my sister and me. My sister and I were never allowed to eat in the dining room with them. We ate in the kitchen like servants and took our plates into the dining room to be filled. This made us feel like outsiders, not like family. I used to think I was beneath the other family members. Whenever they came to visit my grandparents—and there were many of them—I felt a certain shame come over me. They would often come into the kitchen, where my sister and I were eating. They would speak to us and then retreat back into the parlor room. No one seemed to care about how we felt. I could not understand why I felt such shame around them because there was a lot of shameful activity taking place behind those doors at my grandparents, and it was not committed by my sister and me. There were a lot of family secrets that often included non-Christian activities, and they would have an impact on our lives in the years to come.

We were not allowed to watch television or listen to the radio. They actually padlocked the television cabinet and the cabinet where they stored all the goodies (cakes, pies, cookies, and candies). They usually set them out for us to eat when the goodies were going stale. As I reflect on this, I still laugh at how my sister and I would press our noses on the glass of the cabinet, staring at the goodies. One day we found a way to squeeze our little hands into the cabinet and steal little pieces. My grandparents were very strict with us. In fact, we had to sneak to do some of the minor things that came so naturally to other kids. My grandmother could always find work for us to do. Work was her method in raising us, and teaching us responsibility.

There was a man who lived with my grandparents. We knew him as Uncle, though he wasn't related to us. He was a friend of my grandparents, and he paid room and board for his keep. He was a local numbers runner, and it was rumored that he fathered two of my grandmother's children. He was a nice man who took pity on my sister and me because we had heavy housekeeping responsibility at my grandmother's. We had to scrub floors and maintain that large fifteen-room house at a very early age. It was a big house, and there was a lot of floor to clean, not to mention the hardwood floors all over the house that we had to care for. Uncle would get up at about four in the morning and scrub the floors so that my sister and I would not have to. I was so happy he took that responsibility from us. We were proficient in keeping house. We would have to wash clothes and hang them out on the line in snow that was up to our knees. Then we would have to bring them in frozen and thaw them out on the heat grate and then iron them on the mangle (a machine that you feed clothes into and that presses them smooth and gets all the wrinkles out). It was great for sheets and large pieces of clothing. I remember how we had to drag the large area rugs outside and beat the dust and dirt out of them and then bring them back in. My grandmother often took us to work with her to help clean houses. My sister and I became very proficient in the domestic realm. The groundwork was laid for the future. My grandmother truly believed that my sister and I were not going to amount to much. She definitely taught us the value of hard work. That was a lot of responsibility for children between the ages of nine and fifteen.

There is much reflection on my grandmother because she is the one who raised me. I spent the most time with her under her rule, and she had the most influence on my life. The seeds of negativity planted in me had the greatest impact on my early life, and these would follow me into adulthood. My grandmother, though a saved woman, dabbled in witchcraft and astrology. Now don't be surprised. I can hear some of self-righteous Christians saying or thinking, *How appalling! She could not have been a Christian.* Well, read your Bible again. All throughout the Old Testament, God's people sinned over and over again. They dabbled in the occult and every sin under the heavens. So this is nothing new. Even we saved people can fall into traps set by Satan if we are not in right relationship with the Lord and He is not at the forefront of our lives. I can't speak for my grandmother's choices. I feel that she did not know her Bible and that she was walking in ignorance. I know she was saved, and I know she went to church, and she made sure we went to church. She did not push or encourage education for my sister and me, but going to school and church were mandatory.

—⟋⟍—

My grandmother knew that my grandfather, a retired pastor, would not approve of her dabbling in the occult, so she kept it a secret from him. She worked with oils, not of the anointing kind, and she had a small statue of Buddha on a shelf that she burned incense on. My grandmother made frequent trips to see psychics in Center City, Philadelphia. During her shopping trips to the major retailers, such as John Wanamaker's and Gimbel's, in downtown Philly, she would also visit with fortune-tellers and psychics. She used to take us with her on these shopping trips. She would tell us not to tell Granddad. I look at these as some of those rare moments when I wanted to believe that she cared. I would keep her secret.

She used to read the astrology in the newspaper every day. I was impressionable. I admired her, although I feared her. I, too, took an interest in the occult. I started reading the astrology section of the paper. My grandmother included me once in her witchcraft activity. I remember one time when she was trying to get rid of an abusive boyfriend who was dating one of my aunts. She had me steal his jacket, and in the basement of our home, she cut a patch out of it, soaked the piece of fabric in an oil, and put it in a jar. I watched as she performed this ritual. My great-grandmother, whom we called Granny, also dabbled in some of the occult. I used to have to spend the night at my great-grandmother's starting at about thirteen years old. Granny's house was somewhat spooky to us. My older sister used to be the one to stay at Granny's house at night, but my sister ran away eventually, and I had to take her place in staying with Granny at night. She lived alone, and she was getting up there in age. The family did not want her to be alone at night. Granny believed strongly in speaking with the dead. She would often relay to me her conversations with the dead. She often spoke with her dead husband. Whenever she made my bed, she would read the creases in the sheets. She said they would often tell her if someone was going to die. I was scared to sleep in the bed whenever she read the sheets. My granny kept a red light burning in the hallway. She said it was to keep the evil spirits away. One time I witnessed her salt and pepper the tail of a bat she had caught in her home and then burn it in her furnace. The occult influences were all around me.

I've come from a family plagued with mental illness. My great-grandmother, great-aunt, mother, and three cousins all had mental breakdowns and spent time in mental hospitals. My two sisters each had emotional breakdowns. I still believe my grandmother also had mental problems. She was a mixed woman growing up in a time when it was difficult for biracial people, coupled with the fact that she married so young at the age of fourteen. I can only imagine what was going on inside her. I know she had a lot of anger, which she directed at me and my sister. With mental illness running in our family, I have always known this area to be very thin ground for me, which is why when I pray, I ask God to keep a guard on my mind. He has been faithful. It is important for you to know where I've come from to fully understand how I got where I am now and how I achieved victory in my life coming from a very dysfunctional background. In the Bible, from beginning to end, you will find that God did not use any perfect people to do His will. First of all, there weren't any. The only perfect person to ever walk the face of this earth was Jesus Christ, and without Him, we are nothing. We can't fix ourselves no matter how hard we may try.

—⟋⟍—

I remember all the emotional turmoil and abuse my sister and I received at my grandmother's house. I remember all the arguing and fighting, especially when my mother was well and living with us. The joy of having my mother there with us made me feel like I had a family. When Mom was well, she worked and bought us nice things. But the joy was always short-lived because my mom and my grandmother would always wind up arguing, and it would always lead to cursing and fighting. Then my grandmother would end up calling the crisis number at the state mental hospital to have her committed. In those days your family member could commit you. They would come to get my mom, and of course, she did not go easily. My sister and I would witness people putting our mom in a straitjacket, then they would carry her out of the house as she cursed my grandmother with terrible language. No one in the family ever thought to shield my sister and me from this drama. No one cared about the effect this would have on us or how it would impact our lives. This was our mother, the one who had given birth to us, and yet not one family member on the scene thought to shield the two little children from witnessing the altercation. These altercations happened numerous times. I try to remember the fleeting happy moments, but they are overshadowed by the dark moments. I remember thinking how lucky my younger sister was that my aunt had adopted her. My aunt had married a successful businessman, and I knew my sister would live a good life and even go to college.

I would think about my youngest sister who was taken by her father to live with him and his new wife. I thought about how she at least had a mother and a father and how much better off she was. I wanted to escape my grandparents' home, but I feared what may happen. She loved using the threat of putting us away in one of those homes for troubled youth.

My grandmother had her own issues. She was of mixed origin. Her father was white, and her mother was black. I'm sure it wasn't easy for her coming up in those days (early nineteenth century). With everything spoken in our household, I was led to believe that white was good and black was bad. We lived in an Italian neighborhood. My grandmother worked for a doctor, lawyer, and oil company owner. She valued their opinions and their advice greatly. It was no secret that she favored white over black. I would ask for lunch money, and she would scowl at me and say, "Take peanut butter and jelly. The white kids do it." One time my sister brought a friend home from school. The friend was a nice girl who lived around the corner. She was a very dark-skinned black girl. After she left, my grandmother angrily told my sister not to bring that black thing back into her home. I was learning a lesson in bigotry and did not know it. We were never allowed to have friends over after that. I learned that if I had any black friends, I needed to keep them a secret.

My older sister had run away. My grandmother decided she was going to put my sister away in a home for troubled girls. My grandmother always saw my sister as rebellious. My sister was more vocal than me. I was a nervous wreck who would sit on the steps and suck my thumb. The family labeled me *sneaky*. That was probably because I was so quiet and they never knew what I was thinking. I am surprised they did not realize that these children had been through so much and maybe they just needed someone to love them. They needed my mother to sign my sister over to Slayton Farms Girls' Home. My mother refused to sign. I realized then that she wasn't that crazy. My sister decided to run away to look for my father. I remember the night she left. She told me she was leaving. My sister and another girl from school who was also having problems at home were running away together. I remember how sad I felt. I cried because my older sister and I had been by each other's side since we were born. I was now thirteen years old, and my sister was fifteen years old. She could not take the abuse anymore. During the last episode, my grandmother accused my sister of trying to steal her husband. That was the straw that broke the camel's back. Now how crazy is that coming from a grandmother to her granddaughter? That's why my grandmother wanted to put her away. My sister left, and I felt so alone. How was I going to survive? My sister and I used to fight a lot, but we were each other's source of comfort. Our socialization was stunted because we were not allowed to entertain the company of our peers. Family members who came to the house to visit with my grandparents usually did not socialize with me and my sister. That only compounded the feelings of low self-esteem, rejection and loneliness.

I was too afraid to go with my sister, so I did not ask her to take me with her. I thought my sister was brave. I was scared for her, but I admired her ability to do something about this abusive situation. From the outside it looked to the world that we were living a good life. Because my grandparents were so respected in the community, I knew we would probably be seen as rebellious kids who did not appreciate the sacrifices their grandparents made by rescuing them from abusive foster care and giving them the comforts of what would appear to some to be a luxurious life in the suburbs living in a fifteen-room estate. Yes, we ate well and slept on clean sheets, but it was not a home that we could enjoy. Besides, we did most all of the cooking and cleaning anyway. We earned our keep. I often felt that I was hired help and that I was working off my room and board. We were only truly allowed into the kitchen for cooking, the basement for shoveling coal into the furnace, and our bedroom for sleeping. We visited the other rooms only when we were cleaning them. I used to dread polishing all the silver my grandmother owned. It wasn't like there was a playroom for kids. If my mother was not well, we didn't even get toys at Christmastime. I remember coming downstairs one Christmas and looking under the tree. I was so disappointed. There was not one gift for my sister and me. One Christmas when my mom was well and working, she bought us a floor model television and put it in our room, but my grandparents gave it to my aunt. My mother also bought me a record player, and my grandfather took the needle out of it so I could not play it. Now with my sister gone, I just did not know how I was going to handle life in this house by myself. How was I going to get this woman I called Grandmother to see me as her granddaughter? I feared her, but I still wanted her love and approval. I just did not know how to reach her. I felt very alone. I had hoped my grandmother would soften a little by now. One time I looked to my grandmother to show me some kind of affection, no matter how small. She looked at me and told me that she knew what I needed but that she could not give it to me. She told me she had too many. I read between the lines and accepted what she had to say (she was eluding to the fact that she had too many grandchildren to give me the love she knew I needed). The pity I saw in her eyes as she looked at me was what bothered me. My heart knew I would never get the love I so desired from her. Yet she was all I knew. She was my guardian. These were my seeds. I found out I was unlovable by the one person who should love me. I felt sad. I was a young child, and I never heard the words "I love you."

I decided I could not stay in the same house with my grandmother. I was starting to resent her. I was no longer an unaware child. I was at a stage where I wanted and needed her approval, her love. I understood what that meant. I had witnessed family members showing their children so much love. Why couldn't I have that? I wanted to get away from her, but I did not have the guts to run away. Where would I go? This was the difference between my older sister and me. She was reactive and ran from the problem. I, on the other hand, wanted to deal with the problem or find another way around the problems we faced. For starters I needed to get out of the house. I decided to get a job at the local nursing home. I was tired of wearing the hand-me-down clothes of the wives of the people she worked for. I wanted to be more independent, and I wanted to be able to buy my own school clothes. I wanted to wear clothes that were more in line with what my peers were wearing. I was always embarrassed at school because my school clothes were not as nice as those my peers were wearing. I wore a lot of shirtwaist dresses handed down from the wives of the people my grandmother worked for. And I will never forget those ugly brown Buster Brown Oxfords with the ankle socks I had to wear. I used to sneak my sneakers out of the house and change shoes around the corner while on our way to school. As I reflect on that, I can laugh because those were my fun times. I was breaking my grandmother's rules, and it felt good. My grandmother would buy us new clothes, but they were for church. We had to look good for the church folk. I also wanted to be able to buy my lunch at school on the days they had hoagies and steaks. I sometimes got money from my cousin to pay for my lunch on hoagie or steak day. My grandmother would not give me money to buy my lunch. So I decided that if I was working, I could earn my own lunch money, and I could also use this job to get out of the house and away from grandmother.

I decided to get a job at the local nursing home. I arrived at the nursing home and met with a woman who identified herself as the nursing home owner. I remember telling her I was fifteen years old, although I was only fourteen. Yes, I lied. That's how bad I wanted that job. They hired me to wash dishes every day after school. I offered to work on Saturdays as well. The pay was low, but in my young mind, I was becoming more independent. I just wanted out of the house anyway. I was starting to resent my grandmother, and I knew she yielded much power over me. I had seen her put my mother away many times and saw how she tried to put my sister away. I was determined to make sure that did not happen to me. My grandmother had made me and my sister feel like such burdens that I did not want to depend on her anymore. This would be my first step in breaking free, or so I thought. I didn't want her to throw me into a home for wayward girls. At least my grandmother had taught me about the value of hard work. So my young mind thought this job would start me on the road to my independence. My family truly believed that if you did not work, you do not eat.

I worked my way up from dishwasher to laundry person. On Saturdays, when the laundry lady was off, I filled in and did the laundry for the nursing home. You can see already how all the early domestic training I had received at my grandmother's was starting to pay off. I had become proficient in the domestic realm. I was so proficient that they trusted me with a position that was usually reserved for an older and more experienced person. This was clearly God's doing. The work was hard. It was like being at my grandmother's but without the verbal abuse, and the nursing home staff and residents accepted me. There was a very nice cook there by the name of Rose. She was a kind, gentle African American woman who took an interest in me. When she found out that I knew my way around the kitchen very well and that I could cook, she started showing me how to make some of the dishes served at the home. She taught me how to set up the dinner trays and after a while, I began helping the nurses carry the trays to the resident's rooms and feed the residents who could not feed themselves. I loved Rose. She was like a mother figure. She had a warm and gentle spirit. I used to confide in her about the travails at my grandmother's home. She became my confidante. When I was sixteen, I became a nurse's aide at the same nursing home. The nurses there taught me a lot. That was where I became interested in nursing. I admired the nurses in their white uniforms and white nursing caps. This was about the year 1963 when all this took place. Even this joy was short-lived. My grandmother allowed me to keep this job, but she took my paychecks. She told me that I would have to pay room and board wherever I sent. So she took my paychecks to pay for what she called my room and board. My dreams of buying my own school clothes and being able to buy myself a steak sandwich or hoagie for lunch in the cafeteria at school were gone now. One morning on hoagie day at school, I got up enough nerve to knock on my grandmother's bedroom door and ask for lunch money before I left. I felt it was my money. I had earned it. I was not going to be embarrassed anymore at school for not being able to buy my lunch, and I was not going to ask my cousin anymore. I remember timidly knocking on her door. At first, she pretended not to hear me, so I knocked louder. She screamed, "What do you want?" I remember I got very nervous (as she would often make me feel that way). I very nicely but timidly asked, "Grandmom, can I have some lunch money?" There was a long pause. I think I told her that it was hoagie day and that I wanted to buy one. I heard her moving around in her room. I thought for sure she was going to open her door and lash out at me for waking her up, but instead she opened up and gruffly gave me a handful of pennies. Now some of you may say that was mean, and I agree it was; however, I was just glad that she gave it to me. I felt like I had gotten through to her. It was a victory for me. I was not embarrassed to hand over pennies to pay for my hoagie. I thought my grandmother was mean, but I no longer feared her. This was a turning point for me. How could she say no to me asking for my own money to buy my own lunch? She knew I had worked hard for that money, and I asked her nicely with respect.

Education at my grandmother's home was not encouraged. School was mandatory, but homework was not. We did our homework on our own time since housework took precedence over schoolwork. My grandmother seemed to love to flaunt the accomplishments of my cousins, who were all going on to institutions of higher education, but she never encouraged my sister and me. She had already decided we were not going to amount to anything, and she was preparing us for our failures. I soon lost interest in learning, and school became a means of escape for me from my grandmother's home. My grades were just passing.

Now one may ask, "Where was God in all this?" I never asked because I didn't know God at the time. Even though I had spent my early years raised in the church, I did not fully understand what it meant. Going to church was mandatory. We were reminded often that we could not live under their roof without going to church. So church became another means of escape for me. One Sunday at the age of thirteen during the altar call, I answered a stirring in my heart and went down the aisle to accept Jesus Christ as my personal Lord and Savior. I actually surrendered my life to Jesus Christ, and it felt good. I had not been pressured by my family members. As a matter of fact, my grandmother was surprised. This is another time when I acted independently in response to what I felt in my heart. Oh, what joy! Although I had been going to Bible study and Sunday school, I can truly say I never really understood the full meaning of surrendering my life to Christ. There are probably many of you reading this who may feel the same way. As a child, I was so traumatized and distracted that I failed to comprehend what they were teaching me. My grandparents preached a lot of condemnation in their home. They had me so scared of God that I thought I was going to hell just for being a Montgomery. (Montgomery was my father's family name.) My grandparents never taught me about God's love for me. They made me think God was going to punish me for everything because I was born with bad blood. And that was my lesson in fear of the Lord. They never taught me that a fear of the Lord meant revering

Him. To fear Him is to be in awe of Him, to have a deep abiding respect for Him. He was not this mean God who was going to strike me down at a moment's notice. I had so much to learn. My salvation and surrendering my life to Christ was another turning point in my life. It was not just another turning point in my life. *It was the most important turning point.* God knew the path I was going to take and the things I was going to be faced with. He knew I could not face it in my own strength. He knew me in my mother's womb. I am reminded of this whenever I read Jeremiah 1:5 (NLT), which says, "I knew you before I formed you in your mother's womb. Before I set you apart And appointed you as my prophet to the nations."

He knew my beginning, and He knows my end. God has a path cut out for each one of us. We are the ones who fall off the course that God has paved for us. Some of us never get on course because we do not know about God or His plan for our lives. Many of you may be walking in ignorance of the Lord like I did. Some of you can probably relate to some of the situations I have shared with you thus far. Maybe some of you have experienced verbal and emotional abuse in childhood or even at this very moment, which could be keeping you in bondage with low self-esteem and rejection. The repercussions of these powerful emotions can destroy you, if you do not know the Lord. It can stymie your natural and spiritual growth and set you on a path of self-destruction. This book is meant to show you the way out and to tell you of God's unconditional love for you. It's meant to show you that there is not any situation that God can't fix. It is only by the redeeming power of the blood of Jesus Christ that you will have any victory. I had to learn this for myself.

At the age of fourteen, I was molested by a neighbor's husband. I used to have to walk to my great-grandmother's house to spend the night. As I previously mentioned, she was getting older, and the family did not want her to be alone at night. This used to be my older sister's job, but since she ran away, I was next in line. Out of my grandmother's twelve children and about sixty grandchildren, my sister and I were the one's selected for this job. I'm guessing it was because we did not have any parents to fight for us. Grannie's house was spooky. She was clean and meticulous, but it was eerie in there because she did not try to hide the fact that she spoke with the dead. Whenever I was walking to her home, this neighbor would always be out washing his car. I never thought about the fact that his timing seemed coincidental. I just know that every evening when I would pass by his house, he would be out there washing or wiping his car. He would always speak and say hello. I would respond, but I would keep walking too. He was just a neighbor to me. He had a wife and a daughter. It was only a few blocks from Grandmom's to Grannie's house. It was a straight route. There were a long stretch of trees and some dark areas that I had to pass through. One evening when I was walking and arrived at the stretch of trees, a car pulled up and asked me if I needed a ride. I looked, and it was this neighbor. I knew him, and it had gotten dark, so I agreed. I was often afraid walking alone at night, so I did not see anything wrong with accepting a ride from our neighbor. After I got into his car, he made some conversation, but I noticed he was taking a different route to Grannie's house. An eerie feeling came over me, and I suspected I was not going straight to Grannie's. He drove me to an isolated spot and had his way with me. I was so afraid, but I did not say no because he had driven to an isolated place in the woods. No one knew I was there. He could have killed me and gotten away with it because no one saw me get into his car. I never told anyone for fear that they would blame me. I learned that from the time my grandmother blamed my sister for an abusive incident and wanted to put her away in a home for wayward girls. So I kept it to myself. I came to find out later in my adulthood that this man murdered his wife and was imprisoned in a state mental hospital for the criminally insane. I have come to realize how blessed I was to have the protection of the cross over me. I am still alive to tell the tale. I can't say that everything I had endured up to this point did not have an effect on me or influence some of the decisions I would make during the course of my early life, but I can say I was starting to believe my grandmother's curse. I was starting to believe that I would not amount to anything. My grandmother's words still echoed in my head whenever something went wrong. I made a wrong decision to get into that car. It was my fault.

I remember one day my aunt called from Richmond, Virginia, where she lived with her husband and two daughters. She is married to an Episcopal priest. I always admired them as a family. I loved this aunt because she seemed caring. She and her husband always seemed to take an interest in my older sister and me. Whenever they came to visit with my grandmother, they always made sure they came into the kitchen to speak to my sister and me. They would ask us how we were doing. Their home was the one place we were allowed to visit. I was so sorry after they moved away to Virginia. I used to feel that they felt sorry for us, but they also respected us as family. Uncle was so kind and loved to engage me in conversations about my mom.

Well, on this day my aunt called to make all my dreams come true. She called to speak directly with me. She asked if I would like to come to Richmond to live with them. This was out of the blue. It must have come from heaven. Finally, I could get away from grandmother and get a chance at a normal life with people who actually wanted me. I did not hesitate. I said yes. I was so happy. I thought about how different life would be for me and how I would get a chance to go to college like the rest of my cousins. (Even then I wanted to amount to something.) Even as a child, I wanted to prove my grandmother wrong. It also felt so good to know that someone wanted me. For my aunt to call, I must have been on her mind. My aunt and I agreed. She told me she would ask my grandmother. My grandmother was my guardian, so I knew she had to approve. Now remember a while back when I told you I had fleeting moments of joy in my early childhood? Yes, this was one of those moments. My grandmother said no, which meant I could not go to Virginia. This was confusing to me. How can she say no to someone who was willing to take me off her hands? She had always complained about how we were a burden to her. She always made us feel like she did not want us there. So was this a matter of control? She wasn't sending me with strangers. She knew my aunt and uncle lived right. They were great parents, believed in education, and seemed to have no trouble expressing and showing love. What a great change this would have been for me. My heart was crushed. I cried all night. I just couldn't understand how a woman who made it perfectly clear that I was a burden and made it perfectly clear that she could not love me would deliberately deny me the opportunity to go and live with someone who wanted to care for me and give me the love I so desperately needed. I guess it was not part of God's plan. Was I was getting a lesson in motives? What were my grandmother's motives for not letting go?

I used to complain to my cousin about my grandmother as we walked to school. I talked about how I wanted to leave my grandparent's home. My cousin suggested I ask her mother if I could move in with them. I was able to convince my aunt who lived two lots from my grandmother's house to let me stay with her family. I moved my clothing after school one day when my grandmother was not at home. When my grandmother found out, she was enraged. She cursed my aunt and me, but luckily, she did not force me to come back home. She washed her hands of me. I will never forget her harsh words as she cursed me, "Since you call yourself a woman, be woman enough to stay away and don't come back here. You're not going to do anything but lay down there and get pregnant." She cursed me, and little did I know at the time that I would live up to that curse. But why did she let me go this time? Could it have been that she knew that living with this aunt would ensure that what she had already predicted for my life would come true? Then she could say, "See, I told you so." Living with my aunt in Virginia would have meant a better life. I may have turned out a success with that advantage, and that would discredit her notion that I was not going to amount to anything. But living with this aunt who had six of her own children, was divorced, and was more liberal with her children would bring misfortune in her eyes. I liked that they were allowed to watch television, entertain friends, and freely eat goodies (potato chips, cookies, etc.), which were left out for all. This aunt ran a beauty shop that my grandmother had built for her in the basement of her home. This aunt had a bustling business. She had a lot of friends. My aunt was popular, and everyone loved coming to her beauty shop to get their hair done. I took an interest in doing hair, and I soon learned the tools of the trade. My cousins and I often helped assist my aunt in her shop. It was fun shampooing hair and listening to the latest gossip. I felt a great sense of freedom. The fear I had grown to know from life at my grandmother's was slowly eroding away. I was going on seventeen years old, and I felt I was coming into my own (whatever that meant). And so began another turning point in my life.

There was still a problem. The problem was that there was an underlying insecurity at work in me. I knew I was expected to fail. I wanted to show my grandmother that I could make it, but I did not know who I really was or what I really wanted out of life. I did not get to set goals like other kids. I had fulfilled my only goal, which was to get away from my grandmother. She had destroyed my self-esteem and my self-confidence. I did not like what she made me out to be or what she predicted I would become. I was never allowed to think for myself, and I lacked a lot of exposure to what I saw as normalcy of a home life. This left me with much uncertainty and started a new fear.

My aunt allowed her older children to date, and so I soon began dating. This newfound freedom and my naïveté was a combination that would lead to a long line of mistakes. I stopped going to church and started enjoying some of my new freedom. The closest I came to worship was my cousins and I sneaking up to peep in the windows of the Pentecostal church at the end of our street. We loved to hear the drums and tambourines, and I loved to see a woman known as Sister Fannie dance down the aisles. As little kids, we were made to attend Bible school at this Pentecostal church. I loved that they gave us candy after class.

I remember my first prom. It was my junior year of high school. I had gotten up the nerve to ask the most popular boy in the suburban community near where I lived. Almost everyone knew him. He had his own car, and a bevy of females wanted to date him. I only got the opportunity because his best friend was dating my cousin, and I'm guessing he said yes so he could be with his best friend. I never felt that he was that into me, and I wasn't really crazy about him. I thought he was arrogant and conceited. When he came to pick me up, he was late, and he handed me flowers that were dead. This prom was the worst date of my life. My date never danced with me. As a matter of fact, he left me sitting by myself as he went on to party with all the popular people he knew. I was humiliated. I started thinking about my grandmother's word about how "no man would want me." I asked to go home. Of course, asking to go home meant my cousin and her date would have to leave as well. I wasn't trying to be a spoilsport; however, all too familiar feelings of rejection were starting to bubble up inside me, and I wanted to escape from the situation. I wanted to protect my feelings and emotions. I was always the one who kept her emotions in check. No one ever knew what I was thinking or how I was feeling. I had been well trained in keeping my mouth shut. I was raised to speak only when someone was speaking to me. So here was another situation that I accepted, even though I felt rejected, and never let this young man know how he made me feel. We discussed my wanting to go home in the car, and my cousin reminded me that if I went home, she would have to as well. After all, I lived with her family, and we had left together. I think we went to get something to eat after that. I remember this young man coming to see me at my aunt's house several times after that. I began to think that he might actually be interested in me. He asked me out one Sunday afternoon. He arrived in his convertible with music going. I felt special. He was nice to me. He was a little more attentive than he had ever been. I remember the song "Groovin' on a Sunday Afternoon" was on the radio. He invited me to his home. I really felt special. His parents were at their summer home, so we had the place to ourselves. He offered me something to drink from his parents' bar. I accepted. He had really set the stage for having his way with me. Satan was using him. Satan is wily and will sometimes use music and alcohol to seduce you into doing things you are not ready for. That is why we have to be careful about what we listen to. I was living a loveless life under my grandmother's rule, and all I wanted was to be accepted and loved. I wanted to believe that someone could love me.

I knew what he wanted, and I expressed concerns about getting pregnant. He assured me that could never happen because he was sterile. I was gullible. It happened. Almost immediately afterward, I started to feel the rejection coming from him. He had gotten what he wanted, and now he did not want to be bothered with me. This scene continued the solidification of my grandmother's words about no man would ever want me. Unbeknownst to me, I was actually starting to live out the curse my grandmother had spoken into my life. Clearly, words can hurt. I want you to know that you can speak negative things into a person's life, especially children. The seeds of rejection and low self-esteem were planted many years early. I was vulnerable to these types of situations because I did not know the Lord. I wasn't looking for victory, and I couldn't achieve it because, although saved since thirteen, I had no relationship with the Lord. I wasn't walking according to His statutes either. I was walking in ignorance of God and how He could work in my life if I allowed Him to establish a relationship with me. I had unknowingly accepted and was starting to live out the generational curse that was placed upon me. I had protection but did not know it because I did not know the Lord. I must have had some discernment because I sensed from the beginning that this young man had no real interest in me, but I went along with it anyway.

It was the beginning of my senior year when I found out I was pregnant. I was devastated. I never told anyone that I was pregnant. I was in denial. After all, the father of this child told me he was sterile. How could this be happening to me? My aunt and my mother told me I was pregnant. There is a certain look a pregnant woman gets that older more experienced women can see. I had so looked forward to graduating. Again, I wanted to prove to my grandmother that I was going to be somebody. Now I had messed up. What was I going to do? How was I going to raise this child? How was I going to face the embarrassment of being eighteen and pregnant? How could I ever face my grandmother? I had never received love, so how was I going to give love to this child? I had built a wall around my heart to protect myself from further pain, and I had kept my emotions in check. Now what?

Would I now be seen as a failure? The fact that my grandmother had such a profound effect caused me to question my own ability to love. I didn't even know how it felt to be loved, so how could I give it?

Having my daughter actually taught me how to love. When I laid eyes on the life that came out of my body, my whole perspective changed. I loved her. I immediately wanted to possess her. I attribute this to God and consider my daughter a gift from God, no matter how she came into the world. This was going to be my lesson in love. I believe God knew what I needed. I believe He knew His plan for my life. I believe He knew I would not be a useful vessel if I had a wall around my heart. My first lesson involved loving the child I had brought into this world, even though her father wanted no part of me or her. He even denied she was his. That hurt me deeply. I was not sleeping around, and I was not the type who would have accused the wrong man. She even looked like him, but he still denied her. I could see she was going to be faced with rejection like me. The generational curse did not stop at me. However, I was determined I was going to love and raise my daughter myself. Even though he would visit with his parents and bring me money, I did not want him to come. I knew how he really felt, and I wanted no part of him. His parents knew she was their son's child and wanted to be involved in my daughter's life. After all, she was their first grandchild. I had begun to resent them coming to see her because each time they came, they bought lots of gifts, and I knew I couldn't compete with that. My daughter was not for sale. They also reminded me of him and how he had lied to me and how badly he had treated me. I never told them. I knew I would have to leave school and put any dreams I had on hold. I had been taught the lesson of responsibility at an early age. I accepted that my daughter was going to be my priority.

I knew I would have to provide for her. I knew I would not get help from the family. I was appreciative that my aunt allowed me to continue to live with her family during and after my pregnancy. This aunt had a heart. She used to take in stray cats and dogs, so although the house was full, she let me stay. I would pay her for my room and board.

Here I was eighteen with a child. What was I to do? Even at this stage of my life, I walked in spiritual ignorance. I knew nothing about the Lord, and I never considered that God would care about what happened to me. I feared God. I was raised with the notion that God was a punishing God. I was also young and vulnerable. Up to this point, my life had been a lesson in survival.

During those days the state hospital was a place that employed a lot of people. It was a state facility, and state jobs were considered good jobs. Several of my relatives worked for the hospital, and my mother was a patient there. I applied and was hired at the hospital as a psychiatric aide. I was so happy that now I could afford to care for my daughter. It wasn't enough to survive and pay rent on my own, but it was a start. Now I could pay my aunt room and board for me and my daughter. I got extensive training as a psychiatric aide, and I passed all my classes. I was officially in, and I was so glad to be working. I worked through my pregnancy. The sad part was that the building I worked in was directly across from the building my mother was a patient in. I would sometimes look out the window and see her sitting on the bench and smoking a cigarette. This was a difficult time for me, but I kept it together. At least I was close enough to her so I could see her. I was always looking for a positive in a negative situation. Although I was raised in a family immersed in mental illness, there was much I still needed to learn about it. As a child, I could never understand how an argument with my grandmother could end up with my mother being taken out in a straitjacket. I was determined it would not happen to me. They had run the gamut on my mother—electric shock treatments, ice water baths, heavy sedations on every kind of antipsychotic medication until she walked in a zombie like state. All this because someone in the family called and said she was out of control.

—⟋ⅢⲔ—

My aunt started dating a man who had issues. He drank a lot and liked to fight when he was intoxicated. He could make everyone in the house very tense because you could never tell what was going to set him off or what he was going to do. He had fought my aunt on many occasions, and at one point he had put her in the hospital. The situation was volatile, and his rampages seemed more frequent. One night during one of his rampages, he snatched an electric cord out of the socket that was just above my daughter's bassinet. She was only about eight weeks old. I heard her cry. I looked and saw a mark on her forehead. My aunt's boyfriend seemed unconcerned about what he had done. I was furious. It set something off in me. She was mine, and the female lioness in me went into protective mode. He had injured my helpless little angel, and I knew I needed to avenge her injury. I first wanted to get her out of the house, so I wrapped her up and took her to my mother's apartment. Mom was out of the hospital and was doing very well. She had her own apartment and had a job. I trusted my mom with my daughter. I left my mother's and went to the local councilman's home. I ask him what I should do. He advised that I should go down to city hall in the morning and file charges against my aunt's boyfriend. I was not satisfied. I wanted immediate justice. I was seething with anger. I even went to the local pool hall and asked the local mobster for a gun. He refused because he knew my family, and he did not want me getting into trouble. So armed with years of emotional, physical, and verbal abuse, I returned to my aunt's house and confronted the man who had injured my daughter. He hit me, and I fought him with all my might. I remember everything went black, and I unleashed great fury on him. He wound up in the hospital. When he got out of the hospital, he returned to my aunt's home where I was still staying. I remember overhearing him on the phone talking, vowing to get even with me. I became concerned for me and my daughter's safety. I started sleeping with a weapon under my pillow. I soon came to realize that even my aunt had turned on me. I knew I had to move. It saddened me that an aunt who was my own blood relative and a person I respected so much would turn on me, her niece, for an alcoholic, abusive boyfriend. I felt I did what I had to do. I felt I had defended my daughter, who could not fight for herself. My aunt's attitude toward me only reinforced my grandmother's cursing many years before. I knew then that I did not belong in this family. This situation confirmed the fact that no one cared about me or my child. I knew I had to move, but where would I go? I knew no other family member was going to take me in, especially with a child. I came from a family who believed if you made your bed, then you lay in it. I took my daughter to her paternal grandparents and ask them to care for her until I could find an apartment. They agreed. I could feel the road was going to be long and hard. I wanted to protect her from this hardship I felt coming. And so began another turning point in my life.

I was now nineteen years old, abused, confused, naïve, and lonely. I knew about prayer, but I knew nothing about the power of prayer. I was never taught how to pray, and I mean really pray about a situation. I did not have a full understanding of how God worked through prayer. I can remember seeing my great-grandmother on her knees, praying before going to bed. I remember my mother being labeled a religious fanatic just because she carried her Bible around with her and prayed several times a day, and if you happened to be there or be visiting with her, she would make you get down with her and pray. She spoke in unknown languages, and everyone chalked it up as my mom's crazy behavior. I now understand that God was the vehicle to her recovery and that the unknown language was her speaking in tongues. We used to giggle when we visited her and she would say, "Get in here and get on your knees." She would do the praying, and as a young woman, I just closed my eyes and pretended. It makes me smile. The truth is that Mom knew something we did not know. She knew the Lord. This was the extent of my personal exposure to prayer, which in my mind was purely perfunctory. From what I had observed in my family, I thought you went to church, attended Bible study, said amen, and then went back to doing what you usually did, which had nothing to do with the Lord. There were all sorts of things going on that I have since learned were sinful and against God's law. How was I to learn about God in this environment? Where was He? I learned of Him, but I did not learn about Him. Prayer was not yet a powerful force in my life. I came to find out much later in my life that my mother, the prayer warrior, never stopped praying for her children, not even in her sickest moments. She told me how she would call each of our names out before the Lord and pray for each of us individually. She said that God would tell her what each of us was doing. I have come to realize that she did love us and loved us enough to understand what we were going through and who could help us. She knew God would be our protection and our source of strength. She knew who held the power. Although she was labeled a religious fanatic, she knew her prayers covered us and helped us to survive the early childhood trauma. I now realize I had been riding the wings of my mother's prayer. She was a prayer warrior. Although the devil used her mind for a playground, God had her heart. My mother had survived her own trauma through prayer. She, too, had been molested by a family member and a professional outside the family. She confided in me about the professional. She told me she was afraid to report it for fear no one would believe her. Everyone already thought she was crazy. She turned to God to help her survive.

Knowing I had to move out of my aunt's house, I wondered where I would go. I had no place to stay. I knew other family members would not take me in. I knew not to ask. I always wanted to be accepted by them. Like my older sister, I sought some sort of approval. They always saw the negative in us, and they were quick to point it out. I did not want to risk the feeling of being rejected. While talking with one of the young women I had started hanging out with socially, she offered to let me stay at her grandmother's. Her grandmother apparently agreed, and it was decided she would charge me thirty dollars a week. Her grandparents lived in another suburban community in Pennsylvania. Her grandparents were a nice, quiet, Southern African American couple who lived in a small home down along the railroad tracks, which was in stark contrast to where I was coming from. Although they lacked a lot of the material things in life, they were humble and happy. They were well liked by everyone. They had been married many years, yet you could still feel the love and respect they had for each other. Their four-room home was small, but it was tidy and clean. The bathroom was tiny and fit only the toilet and a small sink. There was no bathtub. They bathed in a huge metal tub that they sat in the middle of the kitchen floor and filled with water. The grandmother was a hard worker. She was the strong, silent type who touched my life in a way that made me feel like someone cared. Her eyes were piercing through her dark skin. She could look a hole right through you. Even though I was African American, I had not been around many dark-skinned person of my own race at this time. My grandmother was of mixed origin (Irish father and African American mother). My grandmother was very pale with red hair and blue eyes. She could have easily passed for caucasian. My grandfather was Cherokee and African American. My grandmother had racial issues with dark-skinned people. There were many negative connotations in our house. This was a common theme back then, and I'm sure many African Americans can probably relate. Our own African American race had issues too because of our various shades of color. As a child, I was teased because of my fair skin. At school I was teased that my mother went out with the milkman. My early childhood included bigotry, but I never let that affect me. In fact, I always seemed drawn to people in my race who were of darker complexion.

My friend's grandmother took me under her wing as if she were caring for a lost sheep. She used to look at me with wonder. She was the first person ever in my life to serve me. Her service was unlike anything I had experienced. After all, up to this point I had been fully trained to serve others and to do so without question. She filled the shoes of a mother figure, something I had been missing up to now. She cooked my meals. (She was a wonderful cook too.) She fixed my plate, and she washed and ironed my clothes while I was at work. She even drew my bath and washed my back. I had never had anyone do this for me, and I never took this kindness for granted. I now know God used this woman to reach out to me, to give me whatever it was I needed at that time toward fulfilling His purpose for my life. I had come to appreciate the little things in life. Too often we are so busy looking at the big picture that we miss God when He shows up in the little blessings. God moves in mysterious ways, and He uses whomever

He chooses to fulfill His purpose to give us what we need. I was comforted by the fact that someone seemed to genuinely care for me.

While living out here on my own in this new community, I started hanging out with a new group of friends. We partied and got high on marijuana. I went through a couple of bad relationships. I really did not know what to do with my life. Although I appeared to be having a good time, I was depressed, lonely, and confused. I wanted someone to rescue me from this private state of woe and anguish. I wanted to have my daughter with me, but I was not making enough money to afford an apartment on my own. I used to visit with my daughter. I always wanted her to know who her mother was. I remember crying uncontrollably one night. I decided to take a chance on calling my grandmother. I had hoped she would offer some emotional support. (I still had not learned. I was still seeking her approval.) It was the wrong choice. As I poured my heart out to her, she was silent. Then she angrily spewed, "You're not living right," and she hung up the phone on me. I had been rejected again. How dumb of me to think that her feelings had changed about me. I knew for sure I had no one and would never be able to go home.

I had some bad experiences with the people I called my friends. I had a good heart, and I was naïve. These supposed friends soon learned they could take advantage of my good nature. I was hungry for friendships and would give beyond measure so people would like me. My early childhood training made me a people pleaser. I started to see the light and got tired of people using me. The straw that broke the camel's back came when I was asleep one time. My friends took my car without my permission and went partying in Atlantic City. I was furious. Suppose they had an accident. I would be liable. Did they think about that? I started to realize that they also did not care about me. I started recounting all of the little things they had done to me. I remember a time when I was out at a club in Center City, Philadelphia, I saw my roommate, who was supposed to be my best friend, stroll in the door wearing my brand-new dress. I had left it hanging in the closet with the tags still on. I had not worn it even once. I was filled with rage, but I did not let her know it. I remember the damage I did at my aunt's house whenever I unleashed my anger. I realized I needed to get away from this negativity before I hurt someone. I had pent-up emotions, and if I unleashed them, the person on the receiving end would feel all of the hurt I had suffered in my life thus far. So I decided I would move away from these bad relationships. I was impulsive by nature and not afraid to move away from people and situations that warranted it. I had to protect my heart at all costs. A lot had happened to me between the ages of nineteen and twenty-one. I was moving away from certain people and situations and not looking back. I still had not learned to turn to God in prayer. This began another turning point in my life.

I talked with my mother, who was out of the hospital and doing well on her own. She had her own apartment and allowed me to temporarily move in with her. I made a new best friend who lived in the city. She was nice and employed. She had her own apartment and was looking for a roommate to share the rent. I was still employed at the state hospital, so I knew I could afford to share the rent. I thought I could start to turn my life around now and prepare a place for my daughter and me. She lived in the city, so I moved in with her. I would soon find out that this was another bad hookup. I was a poor judge of character. I was gullible and hungry for friendships. Soon after I moved in, I found out she was about three months behind in her rent and was about to be evicted. I had a little money in the bank that I had been saving to get my own place for me and my daughter. I took that money and helped pay the back rent. I used the rest to help fix up the living room in her apartment because it was empty. I was nice that way. I would do anything to help anybody. I was always seeking approval. I wanted to be accepted and liked. I did not realize it at that time, but as I reflect on why I made some of these destructive decisions, it all seemed to point to my early childhood conditioning. I was raised to be a servant and a pleaser. Years of rejection, verbal and physical abuse, and being told I was never going to amount to anything had taken root in my heart, and the seeds were starting to blossom. While living in the city, my car was stolen. I went outside to go to work and found it sitting on cinder blocks, the wheels gone. The next day they came back and took the rest of the car. What was I supposed to do? How was I going to get to work? The state hospital in the city was more than an hour commute. I commuted for a while, but the journey and the job became too much. I quit, and even though we had paid the back rent, we got evicted anyway. I was twenty years old. I felt very alone and depressed, and now I was homeless. And as usual, I never let anyone know how I was feeling. I used to keep a smile on my face. I had become very good at hiding my emotions. I started wishing I had never moved to the city. The money I had saved was gone, and now I knew I would not have my own apartment anytime soon. I was homeless for the first time in my life. It's a devastating feeling, not knowing where you will lay your head when the night comes. All this, and I still did not think to pray. I knew I was tough. I had been prepped for hardship. And so began another turning point in my life.

My new best friend and I had a small circle of close friends and a large circle of associates, or so we thought. We were able to find someone to put us up for a few nights. There were two of us. Who was going to put us both up? I wasn't working, so I would not be able to pay rent. My roommate was a league bowler at the local bowling lanes. We were able to keep a small bag of our personal belongings in a locker at the bowling alley, but we had to put the rest in storage. No one knew how dire our situation was because we were good at keeping up appearances. We hung out with the middle-class working crowd, and we were too embarrassed to let them know the whole truth.

We used to frequent a club where all the cool people hung out. We would go there and find out who was having a party. Then we would follow the crowd to the party, and instead of partying, we would go to sleep. It was becoming increasingly difficult to find someone to put us up for the night. One guy wanted to put us up in exchange for sex. He took an interest in me. I wanted no part of him, and he put us out. I thought we would either have to go to a shelter or sleep on the street. How was I going to get a job without a permanent home address? It was the dead of winter, and I was tired of my roommate and this situation. I secretly felt she had gotten me into this mess. I know I was the type of person who could easily let go of people and situations that warranted it.

My roommate started dating a man in real estate. She told him about our situation, and he let us stay in one of his vacant apartment buildings owned by his real estate company. It was supposed be a temporary stay since we didn't sign a lease and no one knew we were there. We slept on top of the green trash bags that held some of our personal belongings. We were vagrants. I soon learned the only reason he allowed us to do this was so he had a place to be with my roommate. I soon learned he was married. One night when this man came to the apartment, he and my roommate made a proposition. He knew a gentleman who wanted to date me. I knew what they meant when they said date. I was immediately humiliated. How could my best friend even consider asking me something like that? My feelings of self-worth were already about as low as they could go and now I was being propositioned by someone who I thought really liked me. I would expect it from her friend, but the idea coming her was another thing. My roommate's friend was willing to work with us to find a really nice place, but it seemed to hinge on whether I was going to date his friend. How did this man even know me? Had my friend's boyfriend told him about me? Did he know that I had no job and was out in the street? I still had dreams. I still had goals I wanted to reach, although I was taking the long, hard route. I was making the most of the cards that I had been dealt. All I wanted was someone to love me and care enough to make a home for me and my daughter.

My roommate and her friend tried to sell me on the idea. I gave them a flat-out no. At that moment, I had a flashback from home. They both turned on me and reminded me that I had no job and no place to live (but not in that way, they gave me the street version.) They said that I needed to do something. The implication was that they were not going to put me up any longer if I did not agree. I looked at both of them and let them know I was not going to prostitute myself out to anyone no matter how much money I could make. I was offended. I thought she was my friend. Although I could be found guilty of fornication, I felt that prostitution was a step below me. That was my mind-set at that time, but as I reflect back to that time in my life I have to ask myself, was there really a difference between the two? God sees all sin equally, and the two are closely related, except the prostitute gets paid. I knew at that moment I was going to get away from these two people even if it meant literally living on the street. I felt a little blessed that I was able to stay in this empty apartment because the heat was still on. It wasn't fancy, and it wasn't in the best part of town, however you'd be surprised how grateful you can feel for the small blessings when you are down on your luck. All I had was my dignity and integrity, and I was taking that with me. I told them I was going to get myself together and go to school and get a career. They scoffed at me as if to say that would never happen. They didn't know me. I was a survivor. I started to realize that I needed to make some concrete decisions regarding my life. I still had to prepare a home for my daughter so that I could get her back. I still had not learned to turn to prayer.

I left the apartment that night angry and ready to spend the night on the street. I knew I was truly on my own. I needed to find a place quickly. Here I was alone again with no friends, but I felt I had made the right decision for my own life. I would face whatever I had to. I was not going to turn to prostitution just because I was having a hard life. I wanted better than what prostitution could give me. I was no angel, but I knew I had choices. I felt I had made the right choice this time. And so began another turning point in my life.

It was late. I caught the subway and went to this bar I knew about. I often traveled the city streets without fear. When you don't know the Lord, you don't know fear. I was feeling depressed and angry, and I just wanted to get high on some marijuana. In those days it seemed everyone knew someone or someplace where you could get some pot. Most of the time, you did not have to buy it. People were free with their drugs in the 1960s and early 1970s. They were willing to share if you were there. I knew this, so I went to the bar. I went into the ladies' room, which was a common place to go if you were looking to get high. Marijuana was my drug of choice at this time. I had tried drinking, but I did not like it. Everyone I ever saw drinking booze became an ugly drunk and out of control. I did not want to drink anything that would wield any control over me and bring the worst out in me. I knew I needed to keep my head on. Marijuana and wine were things that kept me mellow, and I could handle that. I just wanted to forget all the hurt and pain I had felt up to this time in my life. I knew if my emotions ever boiled over, they would be destructive, and I could possibly hurt someone then. I had pent-up pain, and I was not letting it go. If only I knew the Lord then.

There were a couple women in the ladies' room smoking pot and snorting cocaine. We shared a joint, and they offered me some cocaine. I had never snorted cocaine before, but tonight I wanted to try it. I was feeling low, and I was hurting emotionally. I was having trouble getting over the fact that I had been betrayed. I snorted it. They could tell I was a rookie. The older woman noticed me right away. She was street wise and knew I was out of my element. She called me on it. She asked me straight up if I was on the street. She was very straightforward, so I responded accordingly by saying yes. She wrote down her address and phone number and offered me a place to stay for a while. God was with me once again, although I did not pray for it. Someone somewhere was praying for me. I don't attribute it to luck that I was able to find a place to rest my head right at the time I made the decision to sleep on the street. Because I was saved, though walking in ignorance, God showed me His unmerited favor and had mercy on me. He did not let me sleep on the street. I did not know the Lord and did not understand the full meaning of my salvation, but He remained true to His Word, which says. **"And the Lord, He it is that doth go before thee; He will be with thee, He will not fail thee nor forsake thee: fear not and neither be dismayed"** **(Deuteronomy 31:8 NKJ).**

This woman was unknowingly going to be another person God would use to help provide shelter for me and protect me as He moved me toward His purpose for my life. This was going to be yet another turning point in my life.

I took this woman up on her offer and moved in with her and her seventeen-year-old daughter. I was still walking in spiritual ignorance and unaware of the power of God in my life. I knew He was there because with every decision I made to get away from a bad situation, a blessing came out of it. I was caught up in a struggle for my survival. This was just another situation I had fallen into that I had to deal with. I never let go of my dreams and the goals I had set to get my own apartment and a job so that I could get my daughter back, who was still staying with her paternal grandparents. These dreams kept me going. I never told anyone. I just knew I needed to survive. I felt like a victim of circumstance.

Moving in with my new friend exposed me to a life I had never known before. My friend lived in an upper-middle-class neighborhood on the fringe of suburbia. She had a lovely home. I remember she asked me about my family. She asked me who she should call if I got sick or if something happened. I told her I had no family and that there was no one to call. I lied. I felt like I had no family. They had rejected me, so in my mind, I had no one I could depend on. Besides, they had never treated me like family, and I had never felt like I had belonged. My grandmother had made it perfectly clear that I was not welcome back at her home. So here I was on my own, striving just to live.

My new friend was married, and I soon found out her husband was serving time in a federal prison because he had been a major drug dealer. Most of her friends were somehow involved in drugs. They were different from people I thought would be involved with drugs. They were middle class, and they lived in nice homes. They dressed well and seemed educated, and some owned businesses. I never stood in judgment of them. I was so glad that they welcomed me into their circle. I was lonely and tired. I'm sure my naïveté showed through. In fact, I would sometimes be the butt of their harmless amusement. They knew I was ignorant of this world in which they lived. Even though I had smoked pot and taken diet pills, I had never been exposed to a life where various types of drugs were so plentiful. (My first exposure to drugs came from home. Most of my aunts were on diet pills to maintain their weight. I started using diet pills at sixteen years old before I left home.) My friend used to tell me I was different, and she always seemed to want to protect me. Their lives were a secret in their neighborhood. There was no overt drug activity in their neighborhoods. I did not fear my new friends. I was always trying to fit in. Acceptance was something that was so important to me at that time. I was suffering with low self-esteem and the effects of rejection. I felt I was the underdog, and I found comfort with people society would see in the same way. Maybe some of you can relate to this.

My new friend taught me how to get my life back together. She was a survivor, and I respected that. She was also brutally honest and outspoken. She had always worked in a bar or a club so she taught me what she knew. She was sixteen years older than me, and though she was my friend, she had become somewhat of a mother figure. I was twenty-one years old. She advised me that I would need to get a job. She was going to start charging me for staying at her home. This was fine with me. I so wanted to get on my feet. I had been taught the art of responsibility at an early age. My own grandmother charged me rent at the age of fourteen, so I had no problem paying my friend for putting me up. She helped me search the papers for jobs, and we soon found an ad for a barmaid and waitress at a nightclub. She suggested I go see about it. She went with me. I had never worked in a bar before, and the closest I had come to waiting tables was from my early childhood training at my grandmothers' house, where I waited on family members when they came to visit. I felt I could handle this. I was hired on the spot. I was so glad that I would finally be able to get a paycheck and start saving for my apartment.

I was making what I thought was decent money, especially with the tips. I was a hard worker. The owner was impressed with my social skills and my bookkeeping, so he promoted me to maître d' and bookkeeper. As head bartender, I kept the books and recorded daily and weekly hours of the employees and submitted them for payroll. I was starting to feel like a whole person again. I was coming to realize my own skills. The club where I was working was a bunny club, and yes, I wore the costume. I never gave it a thought. I was just glad I was working. It never went to my head. As a matter of fact, I could not wait until the night was over to take that outfit off. I was a jeans and T-shirt person. This job did not last long. Many knew that the owner was having a nervous breakdown, and he had a reputation for being eccentric. One of the patrons offered me dinner one night. I was on my dinner hour, so I accepted. It was at this time I found out how crazy the owner was. He got angry and put all the patrons out of his club. He closed the restaurant early and called all the staff into the dining area. He pulled out a gun and dared anyone of us to try to leave the club. He said anyone who walked in front of his gun would be shot. I knew I needed to get out of there. I slipped out of the dining area, went downstairs, changed my clothes, and called a friend. I went back upstairs, walked over to the owner, and told him that I quit. He looked at me as I passed right in front of his gun and out the front door. I never looked back. I sensed he was bluffing, and I did not fear him.

Things were starting to go downhill for me. I was unemployed again. I soon got another job working at another bar. It was a lively and busy place. The salary was not that great, but I made excellent tips, which helped. My hopes were up again. I did not put my money in a bank. Instead I chose to hide it at my friend's house. My friend had taken in another boarder. That boarder found and stole the money I was saving. I was livid. The situation at my friend's home was becoming tense. I knew that if I did not move soon, I might snap and hurt that boarder. I remembered the fight at my aunt's home with her boyfriend, and I did not want a repeat of that. I did not hurt people, but I did not trust my emotions. I had bottled-up pain, and if unleashed at this point in my life, I knew it would lead to destruction. I would rather just move on. I had no personal connection with these people, and it would be easy to let go. This would begin another turning point in my life.

I seemed to be drifting from one bad situation to another. Though I came from a Christian family and I myself was saved, I did not know the Word of God. I did not know the power I had been given through the blood of Jesus Christ to overcome the pains of rejection, abuse, depression, despair, addictions, escapism, loneliness, witchcraft, afflictions, and feelings of hopelessness. The one thing I did have going for me, even though I did not realize it at that time, was the grace of God and my ability to say, "This too shall pass."

In **Genesis 28:15** (NLT), I am reminded of God saying, **"Behold I am with you and I will keep you wherever you go, and I will bring you again into this land. For I will not leave you until I have done that which I have spoken of to you."**

I had come to expect hardship. Hardship was all I knew. It had become my norm. As I reflect now, I realize the path I was taking, though a hard one, was leading me back to God, the only Father I would ever come to know. I can now thank God for the trials and the hardships. It was through them that I found Him. At the age of twenty-one, I had a dream. I saw myself in complete and utter darkness, groping my way through a long, dark tunnel. At one point I was crawling arduously on my hands and knees, trying to make it to a light I saw at the far distant end of that tunnel. I remember halfway through I saw my disciplinary teacher from my junior high school, Mr. Cash. He was cheering me on, imploring me not to give up. The dream ended with me successfully reaching the end of the tunnel and stepped into the light I had seen. I was suddenly in a supermarket register checkout with an abundance of grapes. This dream has stayed with me for many years, and I can still see it vividly as I did back then. It has been my guide. I believe God was letting me know that I was going to go through some very dark periods in my life, but with discipline, striving and not giving up would play a great role in my coming out of darkness, overcoming, and achieving victory in my life. The light at the end of the tunnel was Jesus, and by keeping my eyes on Him, I would prosper.

I did not move from my friend's house right away because I did not know where I would go, but I knew I had to move. So much had happened while hanging with this crowd. One of our friends was murdered. That scared me. For the first time, I was beginning to feel fear. I also realized that that everyone who smiled in your face did not necessarily like you. One night while at a popular club we used to frequent, someone laced my drink with LSD. It almost killed me. I should be dead today, but fortunately, a real friend stopped me from jumping out an eight-story window. I learned later that the barmaid had drugged me. Although she smiled at me and seemed to like me, she had secretly put LSD in my drink when she served me. To this day I don't know why, but I learned a valuable lesson about people. I was learning not to trust them, even the ones who called themselves my friends. I was not a very good judge of character. I was not reading people. I was just lonely and looking for friendships. I did not have any relationship with my brothers and sisters because of the way we had been raised. I didn't even know where they were at that time. I knew I was not welcomed back home. My grandmother had made that perfectly clear. I'm sharing this because I know there are people out there who can relate and I want them to know that they are not alone. When you finish reading my testimony you will know that there is a God and that He delivers those who call upon His name.

As I pondered my next move, I continued to work at the bar. I met a guy who seemed interested in me. I started dating him casually at first. I told him of my experiences at my friend's house and someone had stolen my money. I told him I needed to get away from there as soon as possible. He offered me an opportunity to stay with him. He was separated from his wife and owned his own home. He was gainfully employed and in no active relationship. It was too good to be true, and though it was not love at first sight, I took him up on the offer to move in with him. I saw him as my rescuer. He was nine years older than me. I was twenty-two, and he was thirty-one years old. I thought having a mature working man who seemed to have his life together and owned his own home would help bring stability to my life. It was a bonus that he was thoroughly into me and had been observing me from a distance for a while. He had a chance to scope me out, but I did not have the opportunity to scope him out. My situation was dire, and I needed a place to live. Here I was again in another right now situation with no time to think things through. I had to move, and that was it. I thought, *now I can get my daughter back. I have a place to raise her.* Little did I know that this was going to be a major turning point in my life. The situation seemed ideal. He had a nice circle of friends who lived normal middle-class lives. They were all employed and owned their own homes. They were responsible parents to their children. I thought I could finally live as I had dreamed and make my family proud of me. After all, my family was always waiting to hear from the jail or hospital when it came to my sister and me. They did not have high hopes for us. I just wanted a husband and a home to raise my daughter.

My dreams were simple. I thought I had finally found someone who would love me. It was only the second time in my life that I can actually felt what I thought was love for someone. I had never heard the words "I love you" spoken to me. This would be the first time, and I fell hard.

—ɷ—

Hanging out with this man and his friends made me feel like I belonged. I liked them. We dabbled in recreational marijuana socially. During that era recreational drug use was common even among the middle and upper classes. We never thought we were doing anything wrong. It was a sign of the times. Drinking wine and smoking pot was what we did when we would get together. There was a sense of normalcy about their lifestyles, and I wanted that for my life, so I moved in with him.

I played the role of this man's wife for fifteen years. I brought my daughter to live with us. I felt that I was finally starting to live a normal life. I was no longer under the threat of possibly being homeless. I could get a real job since I now had a permanent address. I was starting to feel some joy in my life. His house was transforming from a bachelor pad where all the guys used to meet to an actual home. I had excellent domestic skills and would put them to work. I was all about pleasing and acceptance. I wanted him to know that he had made a good choice. I did not want to have to start all over again. This time I would have my daughter with me. I knew I had to make this situation work. I could now prepare for school so that I could get a good job.

As the relationship grew, I came to realize that I had very strong feelings for him, and I interpreted this as love. His best friend felt I was the best thing that had ever happened to him. It wasn't too long before I found out why. This man had a secret side that he kept well hidden from me for a while. He had a temper and could be verbally and physically abusive. He had a drinking problem and was a functional drug addict, who would later cross over into using crack and cocaine. He did not show me this side right away. Admittedly, we all indulged in recreational drug use, but later in our relationship, this man took it to a whole new level than what I was used to. If I had been in relationship with God, discernment would have let me know that something was not right with this man. I was always in a situation where I had to make a snap decision for the situation at hand, so I did not have time to thoroughly think through anything. I seemed to always need an answer right now. That's why I call them "right now" situations. This was becoming one of those "right now" situations that I had hoped would bring about change in a good way. I soon found out I was wrong.

He had become verbally and physically abusive with me. It started small and grew through the years. It reminded me of my grandmother's house. There was a lot of arguing and a lot of threats and intimidation. I started withdrawing into myself. I was becoming afraid of this man. But I had learned to love, and I had given so much of my life to him. I wanted it to work. Once again, I felt afraid. I tired of the thought of starting over again. Even though fifteen years had passed, he still felt I was rushing him to the altar. I knew in my heart that it was not going to happen. The arguments and the fights were monumental. This was not the way I thought my life was going to be; however, I was used to being abused both verbally and physically. It was my norm from the time I spent as a little girl in the foster home to even this situation. I kept hoping it would change.

My nerves were shot. I spent much time at the doctor's office. I was on antianxiety pills and had stress-related gastrointestinal problems. Of all the situations I had come through, this was the worst. Why? Because this was someone I had made an emotional connection with. It was someone I felt I loved, but now I also feared him. So instead of leaving, I stayed, hoping things would change.

I was suffering in silence. I never even told anyone, not even our best friends, although it probably would not have come as a surprise to them. I got the feeling they all knew about this side of him long before I came along. I was in denial about how bad it was. I did not want to start over. The road had been too hard.

My doctor told me he was not writing any more prescriptions for Xanax. He advised me to straighten out my situation at home. He said my health would improve then. I thought my situation must be really bad because I had not told the doctor what was going on. He was wise enough to recognize the signs of domestic abuse. He at least knew that whatever was going on was related to my home life. I'm surprised he never reported his suspicions during that time.

Once again, I felt all alone in a situation I had no control over. I lost a lot of weight, and my hair was falling out in globs. My joy had turned to despair. I used to have some quiet moments whenever he was not at home. Quiet moments were something I did not have in my previous struggles. I took advantage of these moments to search my heart. I knew I could not go on like this. The problem was that I did not know what to do or where to go. I knew I could not go backward, and I was afraid of what lay ahead. For some reason, this relationship and this situation really got me thinking. It forced me to reevaluate my life and the direction it was going. As I reflect, I believe God allowed this to happen for that very reason. Now I could evaluate my life and the direction I was headed. I was tired of the struggle for my survival. I was tired of starting over. I was now thirty-seven years old, and my security was crumbling. For years I had been leaning on my own understanding, and it took a long time for me to realize I did not have to do it alone. Even though I was making my own decisions and messing up, I was still under God's grace, and that is the only reason I was able to carry on. I am sure God was not pleased with the life I was leading; however, God gives us free will, and I had not called on Him through all my years of struggle. Sometimes God has to allow some things to happen in our lives so that we will come to realize how much we need Him. The Word of God says, **"There is a path before each person that seems right, but it ends in death" (Proverbs 14:12 NLT).**

I was on that path, but now my eyes were being opened to the fact that I needed to change directions. I felt helpless, and I knew this situation could kill me. I was becoming desperate, and in my desperation I fell prostrate and finally called out to God. I had a Bible in my home. That was standard for all Christian homes. It was typical that one rest on the coffee table of each home in the early days. Mine was not on the coffee table. It wasn't even out. I had not read it since I had bought it, and it had been so long that I didn't even remember when that was. Now I was drawn to read it. I had finally prayed, and I was looking for a word from God. I had come to realize God was the only person who could help me out of this mess I had made of my life. I had tried astrology and fortune-tellers and other New Age things, but all to no avail.

As I started to read my Bible, God responded immediately. He took me to **Psalm 1 (KJV)**, which reads,

> **Blessed is the man who walketh not in the counsel of the ungodly, nor stand in the way of sinners, nor sitteth in the seat of the scornful. But his delight is in the law of the Lord; and on his law doth he meditate day and night. And**

he shall be like a tree planted by the rivers of water, that bringeth forth fruit in his season; his leaf shall also not wither; and whatsoever he doeth shall prosper. The ungodly are not so: but are like the chaff which the wind driveth away. Therefore the ungodly shall not stand in the judgment, nor sinners in the congregation of the righteous. For the Lord knoweth the way of the righteous: but the way of the ungodly shall perish.

The message was clear and certainly not in need of interpretation. I knew God was telling me I needed to change my way of living. I had been living in sin with an unsaved man, and God was letting me know He could not bless me in this mess. What I saw as right living was not according to God's standards. Though lost, I was still one of His children, and when I humbled myself and called upon Him, He answered. He hit me with the truth of His Word. It may not have been what I had hoped to hear, but it was the truth nonetheless. I was being warned to change my lifestyle or die in my sin. As I continued to read the Bible, God's instructions became clearer to my spiritually ignorant self. Who is this God? I wanted to know more about Him. I had always known of Him, but I had never known Him. My family made me so afraid of Him that I thought I wasn't good enough to get into heaven. I was always taught he was a punishing God, so instead of running to Him, I appeared to be running from Him. How many of you can relate to that? You know you are not living right, and so you avoid any and all conversations or situations that have anything to do with God. It's kind of like shutting Him out. We think that if we don't acknowledge Him, He will go away. God calls it conviction. When we are confronted with our sins, we feel ashamed because we know God would not approve of the lives we are living. We feel guilty, and that guilt brings the conviction.

That's proof in itself that there is a God, for without Him, we would not feel conviction. When we are living in our sin, we are doing what Satan wants, and he does not convict. There is no need. He is happy with what we are doing. He only comes after the people who are trying to live a life for God.

I had run the gamut on the works of the flesh—adultery (knowingly and unknowingly), fornication, lust, idolatry, witchcraft, astrology, drinking, drugs, envy, and revelry. I had been abused and misused, and I was confused. All of these were major contributors to what I saw as my downfall. When confronted with my sin through the Word of God, I wondered, *how could God ever forgive me?* Some of the folks I hung out with in my early years were now dead. I knew I was as low as I could go, and I could only look up now. "But there for the grace of God go I." I still believe that if I had not surrendered my life to Jesus Christ at that early age, I would no doubt be dead too. I had stared in the face of death multiple times, and yet God had mercy.

As I continued to read the Word of God, my eyes began to open to my situation. I read about God's love. I knew about Jesus, but never really knew Him. There were a lot of things I did not know or understand about the faith I professed back in 1963 when I accepted Jesus Christ into my heart as my personal Lord and Savior. Although I had never received love or felt loved, I was about to learn about the greatest love of all—the love of God through Jesus Christ. God's Word had begun to come alive and speak to me. I was familiar with some of the most common scriptures early in life, but I did not really know them. To know them is to put them in practice. I had not done that. I had pulled away, allowing my sinful situations to separate me from God. Since I did not know Him, I did not realize I was separated from Him. I just assumed that God would not care about someone like me whose fate had already been determined by her family. They made it seem as if God only cared about those who had whole families (mother, father, and siblings) and appeared to be living right. I had not read my Bible, so I didn't know that God was no respecter of people and that He used imperfect people to carry out His divine purpose and mission for the world. I had heard a lot of preaching about right living, but no one had ever told me how to do it. It's about more than hearing the Word and living the Word. It's about how to get to the point of right living when you are faced with repeated trials and tribulations from the hardships of life. We can read, but we don't get the understanding until our spiritual eyes are opened. A lot of people are reading blindly. We cannot discern the Word of God with the natural eye. Being in right relationship with God opens your eyes to the truth. Being in right relationship means first believing that Jesus Christ is the Son of God and accepting Jesus Christ into your heart by faith as your personal Lord and Savior. There is no other way around it. We need to not only pray but also believe in the power of prayer. It makes no sense to pray if you don't believe what you are praying. We need to confess our sins and repent of them. We need to turn away from those very sins and strive to obey the statutes and commands the Lord has set forth in His Word. You need to understand that we Christians are not perfect, just saved. The Bible was written as a guideline for believers. The bible is our *Basic* Instruction *Before Leaving Earth.*

Turning to the Lord did not change my situation right away. I was going to learn that God moves in His own time and on His terms. The situation was growing more intense and volatile. I could feel in the air that something big was going to happen. My fears became overwhelming. I think I had been expecting instant relief from my situation, not unlike the feeling I got when I would just walk away from a bad situation. But this situation was different.

I had been emotionally invested in this mess. I kept hoping the situation would change for the better. That was impossible because we were unequally yoked. I was saved. This man was not saved. He did not know the Lord and did not want to know the Lord. The Word of God says, **"Do not be unequally yoked together with unbelievers. For what fellowship has righteousness with lawlessness? And what communion has light with darkness?" (2 Corinthians 6:14 NKJ)**

I was beginning to grow in holiness. My Spirit-Filled Life study Bible (NKJV) states that "godly living may result in disfavor with others because it warns of judgment for the ungodly." Godly individuals live by the ethic of love, selflessly asking, "How can I live for the benefit of others?" They are not lawless or sloppy in the way they live. Rather they seek to do right in everything. It also goes on to say, "Holiness requires that we live according to God's standards, not that of the world. Holiness recognizes the serious nature of partnerships and will not enter into them with those who are not believers. Planning a marriage to an unbeliever will produce an unequal alliance that is to be avoided. To experience a happy union, the believer should align with those whose ideals and visions center on Jesus Christ."

2 Corinthians 6:14 makes it very clear that we should refuse to enter any covenant or partnership with unbelievers. It encourages us to live as holy people.

God made it very clear to me that I had to let that relationship go. For some reason, being hit with the truth about my relationship with this man made my decision to go with God much easier. I wanted more in life. Above all, I wanted to live, and I knew that this situation could only end badly. Somehow you just know.

—◈—

In 1977, we were living in a suburban community in Pennsylvania. I took a job working as a clerical worker for the city. Here I would meet my future husband, although I did not know that at that time. I was going through a lot of changes. I wanted to escape my situation, but I was not going to start any relationship with another man and bring him into this mess. It seemed I was growing up and learning; however, I still was not living for the Lord, and I was still indulging in some worldly things, including smoking pot to escape my reality. Four years after I had started working, I got laid off because of state budget cuts. About four hundred of us were laid off. I was devastated. That was my hope for escaping this situation. I wanted to be able to save so that I could get my own place. Once again, I had my own plan. I was laid off two weeks before Thanksgiving. The holidays were sad. When Christmas came, my daughter and I decorated a lamp for a Christmas tree. I was more concerned for my daughter. I never cared about me. I never received gifts for the holiday. My grandmother never bought us gifts for Christmas or birthdays, and neither did this man I was living with. Only once in fifteen years did he ever buy me anything, and I begged him for that. Now you're probably asking yourself, "Why would a woman continue to accept such treatment?" Well, this was my norm. That was all I knew. Abuse and rejection had become my cultural norm. At that time I truly only wanted to be accepted and loved. I had learned the art of servitude and pleasing other people from the time I was a child. I had already accepted that I was not good enough and that my job was to show others that I could be good enough. It was a lie from the pit of hell, but I was living it out.

I was only without a job for less than a year. The girlfriend of one of our friends was a branch manager at a bank. I ask her to help me get a job. I knew I did not have any banking experience; however, my clerical skills were proficient. Working at DPW had helped me acquire more skills. I got hired as a bank teller. I didn't realize it, but God was providing for me in ways I could not yet see. I worked at the bank for three years. The money was not that great for a teller, and I knew I would not be able to afford to live on my own in this job. I was still thinking of how to get safely out of this long-term abusive relationship. I was living in fear of this man.

I remember I was working at the bank, and although I was putting prayer into practice, I was growing weary. My fears had become overwhelming. One day while I was at work, I felt like crying, but I did not want my coworkers to see me weeping. It was lunchtime, and I told my coworkers that I was going for a walk. I did not want them asking me questions. I was in despair and felt alone in my suffering. I was in a self-imposed isolation. As I walked and cried, I heard a voice say, "Go this way." I followed the command, and at the end of the long street, there was a church. I walked up to the red doors, but they were locked. I so wanted them to be open. I made a mental note of the name and location of the church, and I made a point to return for Sunday service. That Sunday, I attended worship service, and when they made the altar call, I went running down the aisle to rededicate my life to Christ and renew my covenant with God. It was the beginning of another turning point in my life. The best was yet to come. God was letting me know that I needed to renew my broken relationship with Him so that He could fix me. It was becoming very clear.

Now don't think things got easier for me. As a matter of fact, they got worse. God had so much work to undo in me and so much work to do in me too, and I was willing to let Him do it. I wanted to try living His way. Now was the time to stop trusting in me and start trusting God in Jesus Christ. I was on the verge of a mental breakdown, and I was consumed with fear. I started attending church regularly, and I took my daughter with me. She was a good daughter, and she was about to start college. I wanted a covering over her before she left. My daughter was goal-oriented and excelled in school. I wanted to preserve that part of her. She hadn't really been exposed to religion—except whenever

I would smoke a joint and then read the Bible with her. I know it sounds crazy, but there was a war going on inside of me. The devil was battling for my soul, and God was not letting him have it. Although other drugs were no longer in my life, I still liked to smoke joints to unwind (never in my daughter's presence) and drink a glass of wine. When I would unwind from all the stress I was under, I would sneak off to another room and smoke. When I emerged, I would find my daughter, and we would read the Bible together. I was proud of her and wanted the protection of the cross over her life. She gave her life over to Christ at the age of sixteen. I now had the assurance that if I died, she would be covered. I knew that God would take care of her. I had kept my abuse hidden from her. Most of the time, it took place while she was visiting her grandparents on weekends.

The physical abuse did not happen that often, but the emotional and verbal abuse was becoming a constant. Along with the threats and intimidation, I knew he would hurt me badly if he felt the need. The first time he sucker punched me, I knew he was making a statement. I also knew he did not want anyone else to know what was going on. I knew that could lead to my demise. I felt responsible because I had joined this man living a life of sin, and now I was trying to pull away. I remember when he told me I was not fun anymore. He got mad with me one time because we were at a party and I wanted to go home so that I could get up in the morning and go to church. The party life had no appeal to me anymore. I was starting to feel out of place, even though these were people we knew. I knew I did not want to miss church, and I wanted to go home. Then he made it personal and said, "Don't do this to me." I wasn't sure if that was a threat that I would pay for later, but I didn't care. When everyone else asked why I was leaving, I flat-out told them that I wanted to go to church in the morning.

Things got progressively worse at home. It had become a battle of good versus evil. This man was becoming a real Dr. Jekyll and Mr. Hyde. He resented my going to church, and the more I became involved in church, the more volatile he became. He had no interest in being saved. He did not want anything to do with church. He wouldn't let me play my Christian music at home. Whenever I would turn it on, he would turn it off. It seemed the Christian music would unnerve him. Could it have been conviction? I would say yes. He was an open vessel for Satan, and the enemy made full use of him against me. I would get up on Sunday mornings and take my daughter and myself to church. When I would come home, he would be upset. He would complain that he had no way of getting around because I had the car. I knew this was just a ploy to try to get me to stop going to church. I was always doing things to keep the peace. I had already experienced what his temper could do. I knew he was quick with his fists. I remember a time when we lived in the city, he took down two young men who tried to mess with him as he was entering a store. I remember how bloody his fists were. When they could get away, they ran from him. I never forgot that. I knew I never wanted to make him mad. I could read between the lines, and I knew that he was not going to let me take the car again. Up until then, I had been sneaking out to go to church. He would be asleep, and I would get up before him and quickly get dressed and leave. One Sunday morning he woke up before me and advised me he needed the car. So now I had a dilemma. I could go to church or please him by staying home so that he could use the car to go get high. I decided on church. I was learning about God, and I was enjoying it. I wanted to know more about this God who had given so much for me. I was hungry for the Word. So I called the church and asked for my zone deacon. The deacon's ministry each had a particular zone in the community they were responsible for. They were there to meet the needs of families living in their zones. I told my deacon about my dilemma, specifically that I would no longer be able to get to church because I did not have a ride. My zone deacon came and picked my daughter and me up and took us to church on Sundays after that. The man I lived with accused me of having an affair with the deacon. I knew this was another ploy to get me to stop going to church, but I kept going. I was getting stronger, and I no longer wanted to be the victim.

As things started to deteriorate at my home, I started thinking about escaping from this messed-up situation. I was learning more about sin, and I no longer wanted to lead a sinful life. I did not realize it, but God was at work in me. He was opening my eyes and changing my heart. As I began to grow in Christ, this man I lived with was sinking deeper into drugs and sin. One of the problems was that he could afford his high. At this time he was a functional drug user. He made good money working in construction as a crane operator, and he had started to pour all his money into his habit.

He started bringing weapons into the house to intimidate me. When I questioned him about the weapons, his response sounded like a veiled threat. He responded, "You never know when you are going to need them." At this point he was starting to look crazy. I sensed that he did not like that I was changing, and yet he felt powerless to do anything about it. He could see the change in me, and I believe he made up his mind that he was going to kill me. When abusers get to the point where they feel that the woman is no longer willing to accept the abuse, they generally decide to kill her. I felt something big was coming, and the more I felt that way, the more I clung to God. I had promised God that I would trust Him with my situation, and I was going to wait. I did not know what I was waiting for exactly, but I just knew I had to trust Him because God was the only one who could give me victory in this mess. He had brought me this far, and I had to trust Him the rest of the way.

One day the man I lived with brought a vial of cyanide into the house. He showed it to me. He was really trying to scare me, and it was working. Although God's Word says we should not fear, I was not at that point yet. I still feared this man. I was not ready to die. When I asked this man about the cyanide, he responded, "I should have had this for my first wife." That sent a chill through me. Now one may ask, "Why didn't you just leave?" Well, anyone who knows anything about domestic violence knows there are many reasons why a woman does not leave right away. I knew at this point I needed to get out of this situation soon. I thought that I had a plan to leave after my daughter left for college. Up until now, I had kept a lot of the abuse from her, and I did not want anything to break out before she left for college. I wanted her in a safe place in case he became violent with me when I tried to get away. The other reason was I wanted to hear from God. If I was going to believe in Him, I had to learn to trust Him. I wasn't sure how God was going to come through; however, I was not feeling Him at that point, and I wanted God to know that I trusted in what I was learning about His Word and His promises. I was afraid, but not afraid enough to skip out on my promise to trust God. I had been praying, and I was learning to wait on the Lord. I knew I would know His voice, and if He told me to go, I would. To go out on my own would be like repeating the mistakes of my past. My days of impulsive decision making were over, and I felt that it imperative that I trust God in this situation. I knew Satan was mad at me. I was no longer serving him. I desired the Christian life, and Satan was setting his demons loose on me. He had a good vessel in which to do it too. He was going to use this nonbeliever with whom I lived to try to take me out. Sometimes when you make a decision for Christ, things get worse before they get better. And that is the time when you must put all your faith in God through Jesus Christ, our Savior. I was at that point.

I prayed over this situation night and day. I wanted God to deliver me from it. I no longer wanted to live like that. It was very dangerous ground and fast becoming a battle of life and death both physically and spiritually. It was imperative that I trust the Lord. It would be the first of two supernatural experiences I would have with the Lord. I did not know it at the time, but God was going to use this situation to test my faith and teach me to trust Him. I had envisioned a disastrous end to this relationship and was prepared to accept all that it entailed, even unto death. I had finally gotten to the point where I said, "If I die, I die. It will still be a way out of this living hell." Can you imagine living in a situation where even death would be a welcome relief?

—⚊—

I have come to learn that God's ultimate goal for us is to make us like Christ. As we become more and more like Him, we discover our true selves. We discover the people we were meant to be.

I wanted to become a child of God. I know I was saved, but becoming a child of God held much more for me. I wanted to know Him and to feel His peace and above all, His love. I no longer wanted to live a sinful life. I was hungry to know more about a life in Christ. I was broken and battered and in need of much repair. My self-esteem was so low I could no longer keep up the front. God had already started peeling back the layers, and my sin was ever before me. This was not something I could fix. It was more powerful than me, and it was not going to be something I could just walk away from. I needed to confront my sin. I was tired and feeling very alone in my situation. I felt I had brought this on myself. I thought I was doing right by coming in out of the world, settling down, and making the home life I had always wanted. I never thought it would turn out like this. I remembered my days of homelessness and how determined I was to never find myself in that situation again. I told myself I would always have a roof over my head. The problem was that I was leaning to my own understanding and had not consulted God before making any decisions. **Judges 17:6 (NLT) states, "The people did whatever was right in their own eyes."** Well, I was on that road. It led to confusion and self-destruction. I had not submitted to God, and I ended up doing what I thought was right at the time. I have since learned that to know what is really right and to have the strength to do it, we need to draw closer to God and His Word. Although I had accepted Jesus Christ as my personal Lord and Savior and received the gift of salvation and I was coming out of what was supposed to be a Christian upbringing, I knew nothing about the Lord. What little I had learned had dissipated under the many years of hurt, humiliation, rejection, and abuse. I did not know how to draw close to God because I unknowingly was running from Him. I was taught that God was a punishing God. When we did something wrong in our family, we were told, "God is going to get you. God don't like ugly." I was unconsciously afraid of God's disapproval and punishment because of my lifestyle. Furthermore, I was so busy trying to survive that I didn't even think to turn to God. As I reflect on the situation, I realize I was not in a relationship with the Lord. I was just saved, and that salvation had been my survival all along. I just did not know it. I was too busy handling things. How many of you saved people can relate to this? I was learning that I needed to be in right relationship with the Lord to gain the victory. Trying to gain the victory in my own strength was not enough. I was powerless without the help of the Holy Spirit.

Things continued to deteriorate in my live-in relationship. I continued to seek God's guidance. I knew that He was a God who was true to His Word and that He was going to deliver me in His time and on His terms. I had gone through so much in my life, escaping death on several occasions. Waiting on God was not really any harder than what I had already been through. After all, He was God. He was the one who was bringing me through, even though I was not deserving.

I continued to pray and worship God. I stayed in church and started to serve on various ministries. I never told anyone at church about my home situation. I trusted God, and as I studied more about sin, I became increasingly embarrassed to let anyone know I was living in sin. I shared small bits of information with my zone deacon, but I was not completely honest with him about my whole situation. He just knew that there were things going on, and he volunteered to help if I needed it. I did not want to bring anyone into this volatile situation. I did not want any innocent person to get hurt. It was my mess, and I would deal with it. In short, I was prideful. No one ever knew what was happening because I hid it well. I made sure I always looked like I was making it. I had learned to hold my head high even though I was sinking deep in sin. My family had always treated my siblings and me as if we were outsiders, so I had adopted a persona to help me cope. I would later learn that it was pride. I was hiding under the grimace of my sin, and my pride would not allow me to admit that I was failing. I kept trying to make things work until they could not work anymore. Anything that's not done in Christ will not last. Sometimes we try to put a Band-Aid on a hemorrhaging wound and think that will stop the cut from bleeding.

One night I awoke to find the man I lived with sitting in a kitchen chair at the foot of the bed, staring at me in the dark. It was about three am in the morning. I knew this was not normal.

I was a little unnerved by the behavior, but I was not going to let him know he was scaring me. He had a strange look on his face, and his eyes were cold. I listened as he told me that he knew I was planning to leave him, and he went on to describe it as "the handwriting on the wall." He started using expletives to let me know how he felt and what would happen if I did leave. He was no longer using veiled threats. He straight-up told me that he would kill me. I knew by the look in his eyes that he meant it. I remembered the cyanide and the hunting knife and the gun along with the African spear he had been bringing into the house. I was sure he would use one of them. He hung the spear on the living room wall so that I could see it. I had stopped drinking water at home because of the cyanide. I would go to the market daily and get bottled water. I would make sure I drank it all because I did not know if or when he was going to put it in my water. I had become his prisoner, but my hope was still in the Lord. God has promised to deliver me, and I was going to trust Him no matter how bad it got. I needed to hear from Him this time before I left another situation. If I left now, I had no idea where I would go, what I would do, or how I would get there. I was totally dependent on God. I had no resources. I had just started a new job with the military. I knew I could not afford to lose it now.

I was able to convince this man at that moment that he was wrong. I could have gotten an academy award for my performance. I wanted to live another night, and I would do whatever I had to do to make sure I did. God was still working with me and in me to teach me to trust Him, and I had promised Him I would wait on Him. I had not yet heard His voice. My faith was at work. As my fears grew, my trust was slowly eroding. I started feeling that maybe I had been so sinful that God would not come through for me. I knew I did not deserve anything good from God as I had not been living up to His expectations. I was ashamed that I, a saved person, had been living such a sinful life, so it would not surprise me if God decided not to deliver me. I felt I deserved whatever I had coming, and I wanted deliverance so bad that I was willing to accept whatever it was as long as I was out of this situation even if it meant death. I wanted to live the life God originally planned for me. I wanted change, and it could not come quick enough.

The day after that man told me he would kill me if I left him, I exhorted the Lord to come quickly. I was so tired that I could not spend another day in this agony. It was quickly becoming a very dangerous situation. I would not eat because I was afraid he had put the cyanide in my food. I started lighting candles before I prayed, and I had started soliciting the prayers of an evangelist and well-known radio pastor who sent me a prayer rug. I was praying three times a day, pleading with God to come quickly. I started planning my own escape. I did not realize that God's plan was already in effect. Fear had set in and had started to control me. I remember falling prostrate on the floor before the Lord. I remember exhorting Him to release me from my self-imposed prison. I started searching the Bible for scripture to support my despair, and the Holy Spirit led me to **Psalm 143.**

This psalm was my saving grace. After reading this psalm out loud, I knew the Lord heard me.

> **Hear my prayer, O Lord; listen to my plea! Answer me because you are faithful and righteous. Don't put your servant on trial, for no one is innocent before you. My enemy has chased me. He has knocked me to the ground and forces me to live in darkness like those in the grave. I am losing all hope. I am paralyzed with fear. I remember the days of old. I ponder all your great works and think about what you have done. I lift my hands to you in prayer. I**

**thirst for you as parched land thirsts for rain.
Come quickly, Lord, and answer me, for my
depression deepens. Don't turn away from me
or I will die. Let me hear of your unfailing love
each morning, for I am trusting you. Show me
where to walk for I give myself to you. Rescue
me from my enemies, Lord; I run to you to hide
me. Teach me to do your will for you are my
God. May your gracious Spirit lead me forward
on firm footing. For the glory of your name, O
Lord preserve my life. Because of your distress.
In your unfailing love, silence all my enemies
and destroy all my foes, for I am your servant.
(Psalm 143 NLT)**

As I read this scripture, my fears began to dissipate. That day
I knew that God was going to come through. David, the psalmist,
said it all. This psalm ministered to my very need. I could not have
formed the words any better. My heart was in such despair and
badly in need of repair.

The Bible reminds us in **Isaiah 40:31** that if we put our hope
in the Lord, He will renew our strength. The Bible also reminds
us that when we confess our sins, the way is open for God to
bring good from a bad situation. We must repent and seek God's
forgiveness. Then He can use our sin for a good purpose instead
of its original evil intent. He can use what was meant to harm us
and turn it into a victory for us. I would soon learn this lesson.
God had a plan for me, and I was learning to walk by faith. It was
a lesson God truly needed me to learn if I was going to trust Him.
I needed to walk by faith and believe that God was going to do
what His Word said he would do. God's Word promises, "I will in

no way leave you or forsake you." It was the first time I was feeling overwhelmed and fearful of my situation, and I knew I needed a power much greater than mine to deliver me from this mess. For many years I would just walk away from a situation and not look back, but this time it was different. There was something I had to learn about this relationship I had invested so much time in.

It was May 31, 1987, when God brought everything to a head. The man I lived in sin with for fifteen years of my life had decided he was going to carry out his plan to kill me. What he did not know was that God had a plan of His own. This man was not saved, and he did not know God. He was witnessing my life changing for the better, and he knew that he no longer fit into my life or God's plan for my life. He was a drinker, and smoked marijuana; however, he had started using crack cocaine now. He went from recreational use to daily dependence. He did not think I knew about his problem because he hid it from me. But I was able to decipher how heavy his drug use had become because he was no longer bringing his paycheck home. He used this drug away from the home. He was still functional and still able to work. He had been spending more and more time away from home because of his drug dependency, and that was a blessing for me as I drew closer to the Lord. I would dread when he would come home because I knew it was going to turn into something volatile. The combination of the drugs and the booze was lethal. I used to cringe when I would hear his key in the door. Because I feared him, I would put on an act as if everything was okay, but even Satan could read the handwriting on the wall. Yes, I was planning to leave, but I didn't want him to know that.

It was the Memorial Day holiday. That evening he took me out to dinner. I got the feeling it was supposed to be my last supper (no pun intended). He had a strange look on his face, and there was an eerie calm in his voice. His eyes were distant. He took me to a restaurant in Center City, Philadelphia. As I reflect, I can clearly remember this night. The eeriness of his calm attitude scared me. I had gotten used to the loud arguments. This was something new. At the restaurant he told me to get whatever I wanted. He said he was not hungry, so he did not order anything. Now imagine someone inviting you out to dinner and then saying he wasn't hungry. So he just sat there watched me eat. I very quickly lost my appetite. He was staring at me strangely. It was almost uncomfortable. I felt in my heart that this was going to be the night he carried out his plan to end my life. We left the restaurant, and as we walked along the city streets, he just kept staring at me. I would turn away, and when I would look back, I would see a smirk on his face, one that he would quickly hid with a fake smile. It was as if we were playing cat and mouse. I remember we passed a policeman walking the beat. I wanted to say to the policeman, "This man is going to kill me tonight," but strangely, my spirit was quieted. It was a strange and quiet ride home with him occasionally turning to glare at me. I tried to make conversation, but it was not working. He was like a man on a mission. What I did not realize was that because this man had rejected the message of Christ and salvation, he had become an open vessel for Satan. And Satan was using him against me because he was angry that I wanted to live a life for Christ. It was true spiritual warfare. What I have learned is that Satan does not come after those who are living a worldly life of sin. He comes after the people who have made a decision to commit to godly living according to God's commands and statutes. Satan's job is to destroy their testimony. First Peter 5:8–11 tells us to be on the alert for Satan. Satan is our enemy, and he spends his time roaming around, looking for someone to destroy. God commands us to stand firm against Satan, using the strength He has given us through our faith. God promises that if we do this, He will support us, strengthen us, and restore us. God also promises to put our feet on a firm foundation. We arrived back home, and as we approached our front door, he started singing a song quietly under his breath. I strained to hear what he was singing. I heard part of what he sang. "You cheated. You lied. You betrayed me. And now you are going to pay." I could have turned and tried to run at that moment; however, I had promised God I was going to trust Him with this situation, and I knew He was not going to let me down, so no matter how things looked, I was prepared to meet whatever was to come head-on. I was determined to trust God, so I waited. For some reason, I knew I would know His voice when He spoke with me. My spirit was telling me that I had not yet heard His voice. In a volatile, dangerous situation like this, you'd better believe I was trusting God. I remember saying to myself, "If I die, I die. I'm still out of here, and either way, I will be free."

—m—

Upon entering the house, this man put all the locks on the door, including the deadbolt, which needed a key to lock and unlock from the inside as well as the outside. He was still singing his sick song under his breath. It was about 3:00 a.m. in the morning when we went into the bedroom to prepare for bed—or so I thought. When I got to the bedroom, I noticed he had taken the gun and the hunting knife out of the lockbox and had laid them on the nightstand next to his side of the bed. I knew then what his plan was. He had taken these things out before we left for dinner. I don't know how I missed that. My heart started racing as I knew what he was going to do. I was still waiting on the Lord. I knew I would know His voice, and I would wait for Him to tell me what to do. I started imaging the newspaper headlines and what people would say. Surprisingly, I felt calm. I was not compelled to run. I just knew for sure that tonight I would be delivered from this situation, and I was prepared to die. I knew this man no longer cared because this was the first time he ever smoked crack in front of me. He picked up the pipe and proceeded to light it. He had even prepared that ahead of time. I had no doubt he was on a mission to destroy me. I was standing on the opposite side of the bed directly across from him. As he raised the pipe to light it, he glared at me, and I came to realize that I was standing face-to-face with my enemy. The man I had come to know and love was no longer there. Satan had completely entered his body. I could see it in the eyes. I was given the opportunity to witness the evil one. Then I heard a voice clearly say, "Confront your enemy." A boldness came over me as I looked at him and asked directly, "Are you planning to kill me tonight?" I already knew it, but I needed to hear it. I believe God wanted me to hear it.

He responded by saying yes in a voice that was laced with evil. It quickly became very clear to me that Satan was angry with me for no longer serving him. I had made the decision to serve the living God and had no place for Satan in my life. I had served Satan well, especially when I dabbled in the occult, including astrology, psychics, and witchcraft. At that time, I did not know this was an abomination against the Lord. I had learned this at home. I had committed so many other unrighteous acts of the flesh. Now that I had made a conscious decision to follow Christ, Satan felt I had betrayed him, and he wanted to take my life because that is what Satan does. What he forgot was that I never belonged to him in the first place. As messed up as I was, I was still a saved child of God through the blood of Jesus Christ.

At that very moment when this man said yes, a gush of wind entered the room. (I believe it was the Holy Spirit.) There were no windows open either. The force of the gush of wind was so great that it threw me against the dresser. In my haste to catch my balance, my hands landed on the keys to the house. I heard the voice clearly say, "Take the keys." I picked up the keys as instructed, and without question, I started to make my way out of the bedroom. I did not run, and as I looked over at the man I had been living with, he was suspended in time, unable to move. I knew then that I had finally heard the voice of the Lord, and He had come through for me right on time. There was no question I was being delivered from the hands of Satan. As I walked out of the room, I felt as if I was being carried. As I descended the stairs and exited, I heard the voice say, "Do not look back." I remember walking and wondering what I should do now. There was no panic, and as I walked, I giggled. I was barefoot, and I only had a dress on my back. I knew without a doubt that God had answered my prayer and had delivered me. If I had gone by my plan, I would have at least packed a bag and made sure I had my makeup with me. I never leave home without a bag. I sat on the steps of someone's home and said, "Well, Lord, what next?" At this point the Lord told me to go to my best friend's home. She and her husband lived in the same complex as we did. They had just purchased a new home, and a glitch had held up the signing of the papers. So they had not moved yet. I have no doubt God was at work here. God knew He was going to deliver me from that situation, and he knew when and what time it was going to happen. He knew I was going to need shelter, and this was His way of providing it for me. Showing up at my friends' home at that time of morning, they knew what was up. Her husband invited me in and told me I could sleep on the sofa. He said we would figure out something later in the day. I was comforted by this because I had sworn that I would never end up in the street again. It wasn't my roof, but it was a roof nonetheless. I was learning to trust God. I had no doubt He would take care of me. I was not dead. I was still alive, and it was all because of the grace of God. I take no credit for anything.

It did not take long for this man to figure out where I had gone. God had held him long enough to provide protection for me. He soon showed up at the door of my friend's home. He wanted me to come out so that he could talk with me. He started trying to open one of the windows at my friends' home, and they advised him to stop. When he didn't, my friends called the police. The police arrived, and he explained to them that he just wanted to talk to his wife (meaning me) who was inside. He was repentant and apologetic, but I wasn't fooled. I remembered what I saw in our bedroom of the apartment we shared, and I wasn't fooled. I had come to know Satan's tricks. I no longer trusted this man. Discernment kicked in. God had just freed me from this nightmare, and I was not about to walk back into it, no matter what. I would rather die than live in sin again. I had made up my mind that I wanted what God wanted for me, and I knew that life with this person wasn't it. Two police officers arrived. I stayed inside my friends' home and refused to come outside. I truly did not trust this man even with the police there. One police officer came inside to interview me about the situation. He quickly saw it as a routine domestic call. The other officer came in, and he, too, asked me about the situation and what was going on. I told him everything, even about the weapons and drugs they could find back at the apartment. This officer was very nice with warm blue eyes. He asked me, "Is it really over"? He told me about the many times they had to rescue women from these abusive situations only to see the woman wind up back with her abusers. I assured the officer that I was serious and that this situation was definitely over. The officer went to his patrol car and brought back a card with a phone number on it. He advised me to call the number on the card and assured me the people who answered would be able to help me. Later that morning I called the number. It was to a shelter for battered women. I spoke with a woman on the phone who asked me if I knew someone who could drop me off at a pickup spot they designated. My friend took me to that spot. I was not allowed to know where I was going. That way, I couldn't' tip anyone off about my whereabouts. My friends and family could not even know. This was all for my safety, and they took great pains to make sure I was safe. I called my daughter, who was away at college then, but I could not tell her where I was. I assured her I was safe. I was happy that she had not been there during this ordeal and that she was safe. They took back roads to the shelter so that I did not know where I was going. I remember arriving at the shelter, and as soon as I got there, I broke down and cried my heart out. The people at the shelter were so nice and understanding. They assured me everything was going to be all right. I took time out from my crying to let them know that my tears were tears of joy. I was so relieved to be out of that situation, and the tears were a reflection of that relief. Here I was again in a homeless situation, something I promised myself would never happen again. Only this time it was different. I was happy, not sad. I felt free, and God had provided a way of escape just as He had promised. Although the roof over my head was not my roof, it was better than any roof I had ever had. I was covered by the blood of Jesus, and I was so thankful. I expressed concern to the shelter about my job. I told them I had only recently started working at this job and did not want to lose it. I would need to work to support myself. I wondered how I was going to get to work when I did not even know where I was. They asked me where I worked, and I told them I worked at the military base. The shelter staff assured me not to worry because all I needed to do was walk down to the corner and catch the bus. They said it stopped right in front of the military base. I was in awe. I could now see that God had a plan for me long before all this happened. He knew it was going to happen, and He prepared in advance for my protection. The new job was no accident. I had already spent so many years hoping to get a steady job. I knew if I left that man, I would need to be able to afford to pay my own rent and survive. I did not realize that God was already making plans for me. With this job, I also had the protection of the military because no one could get through the front gates without authorization. This job was all part of God's plan for me. I now realize why I never discussed this job with the man I lived with. He never knew much about it and never asked.

I was starting to see how God was moving—all because I trusted Him. Throughout the Bible, we are taught to trust God—not just sometimes but during the good and bad times too. Genuine trust in God says, "Whatever mess I'm in, my heavenly Father will lead me. No matter how overwhelming the situation or how low it makes you feel, God can draw you back into the light. Trust overcomes fear, depression, and hate." I was not worried, and even in this situation I would continue to pray and serve Him. God's plan was fully in motion, and from that day forward, I never had to worry about another thing as God had everything in place. He had been waiting for me to let go and let Him take the reins of my life. I was in awe of watching His plan unfold before my eyes. This was a major turning point in my life. After all those years of struggling to discover who I was and come into my own, it was finally happening. I knew God had His work cut out for Him. There were many layers of negative early conditioning and secular living that led to the many mistakes I had made up to this point. I knew God would be pulling them back one layer at a time. I was truly learning to trust Him. The Bible says, **"So if you are suffering in a manner that pleases God, keep on doing what is right and trust your lives to the God who created you, for He will never fail you"** (1 Peter 4:19 NLT).

I stayed at the shelter for thirty days. While I was there, I continued to serve God. The same bus that took me to my job also stopped at the corner of the street my church was located on in Jenkintown. Again, I was in awe of how God's plan worked together for my good. He planted me in a church and a job that he knew I could easily get to even before I knew I would need these. It was all part of His perfect plan for my life. He planned this well in advance. He knew what I was going to need. I was able to get to church and work worry-free.

While at the shelter, I ministered to the women there about their situations. Many of the women were amazed at how I was able to quickly let go of my situation. They shared their stories, and yet some of them were sneaking out to meet the very men who had put them there. I was able to help two of the women get jobs at the military base where I worked. I was determined to help as many as I could. I wanted to give back after God had saved me and shown me His grace and mercy. I promised God I would serve Him the rest of my life, and I meant it. I had lived the true dangers of domestic violence just like the women I now shared a house with. I knew I had learned a great lesson, and I wanted the women there to know who had helped me and how they, too, could receive God's love and help. I knew that with what God had allowed me to witness in that apartment on May 31, 1987, He had a bigger plan for my life. The Holy Spirit at work on my behalf is forever etched in my heart. I knew there had to be a reason for my supernatural experience with the Lord, but I was not asking questions. I decided I would just follow God's lead. The only thing I was afraid of was failing Him. I was finally learning about the God I had surrendered my life to at the age of thirteen. I had been a saved individual with no personal relationship with the God I had asked to save me. Without a personal relationship, you can easily fall. Even Christians aren't infallible. Now I realized the importance of being in a close relationship with God through the blood of Jesus Christ. After witnessing His powerful works and how He had saved my life in more ways than one, I wanted to know more about Him. I was hungry. He was no longer a God who seemed far away. I had come to realize He was real and He was alive.

I stayed at the shelter for thirty days. I continued to witness how God was working on my behalf. As my thirtieth day was approaching, I prayed and ask God about where I should go. I had not yet started to look for an apartment. I had lived with people all my life. This would be the first time in my life that I would actually be apartment hunting for myself. I had no credit history because I never had any credit, and I had no rental history. I was blessed that God had kept me employed most all of my life, so I had a work history. My salary was not the greatest because I had just started this job with hopes of advancing, but I had to find a place to live. I was learning to consult with God first. There would be no more impulsive moves. This move had purpose. Then the Holy Spirit spoke to my heart. He reminded me of the apartments across from the military base where I worked. I remembered how I used to stare at them every day as my friend and I passed by going to work. They looked nice. At that time with so much going in my life, I could never imagine living there. They seemed so out of my reach. I was sure the rent was above what I could afford. But I had taken an interest in them the year before. I would just stare at them. When the Holy Spirit spoke to my heart, I was reminded to trust God. Why wouldn't I trust Him? Look at what He had already done.

I talked with my counselor at the shelter and advised that I was having difficulty finding a place to live. I asked what would happen to me if I could not find an apartment by the thirty-day deadline. She advised that they could give me an extension on my stay if I needed it. It was a few days away from June 30, 1987. I once again prayed and expressed my concerns with the Lord. The Holy Spirit moved in my heart and told me to go to the apartments across from my job. I made an appointment to meet with a woman named Lorraine, the leasing agent. When I arrived, she greeted me warmly. Right away she said, "Have I got the apartment for you. You're going to like it." I thought we were going to discuss my income and where I worked first, but she took me right up to the apartment. As soon as my feet stepped on the carpet, I knew the apartment was mine. I just knew that this was the place God had chosen for me long before I knew I would be living there. Lorraine escorted me back to the leasing office. As we walked, I thought, what should I tell her? Will my coming from a shelter hinder my chances of getting accepted? I knew I did not have any money in the bank. All I had was my paycheck. How would I be able to put down the deposit? It wasn't payday. I heard the Holy Spirit in my heart say, "Be honest." So I swallowed my pride and told Lorraine that I was coming from a women's shelter. She looked at me with a warm, nonjudgmental smile and said, "Will you let me speak for you?" She further advised that the complex was owned by men who would say, "We didn't want that kind of thing happening here." Lorraine advised me she would take care of everything. For some reason, I trusted her. I was feeling hopeful. Two days before I was due to leave the shelter, I got a call from Lorraine when I was at work. She said, "I have good news and bad news. Which do you want first?"

I ask for the good news first. She advised that I had gotten the apartment. My heart was full of glee. I said, "Praise the Lord." Then I asked her, "What's the bad news?" She advised me that the owners wanted the first and last month's rent, but they also wanted an additional $450.00 security deposit. She asked if I could get the money to her soon. Then I could pick up my key. Without thinking, I said that I would get her the money. The call ended, and I immediately started wondering how I could get all of that money together. I went to my church and asked. The deacon's board gave me a check for $450.00. I had saved one paycheck in the bank, but I still needed $450.00. I remember discussing this with one of my best friends and coworker. She was so happy for me. She told me she and her husband had just gotten their income tax refund and that she would give me the money I needed. She said I could pay them back on payday. See how God works? Who could doubt that there is a God? In the matter of two days, I had all the money for my move-in, and it was right on time for my move out of the shelter. God is never late, and He is always on time. He had this in His perfect plan from the beginning. He knew what I was going to need, and He set it in motion. Now I know some naysayers will probably call this coincidence. I call it God at work. The day after my move-in, I went to the rental office to thank Lorraine for working on my behalf and helping me get into the apartment complex. There was a man behind the desk, and I asked him if Lorraine was available. He looked puzzled briefly as if he did not know who I was talking about. I told him she was the nice lady named Lorraine with whom I had signed the lease. He replied that she was a temp and was no longer working there. It was in that instant that I realized God had sent one of His angels to war on my behalf. She interceded for a brief time, and when her assignment was over, she was gone. No one can tell me there is not a God. I feel for those who don't believe. I know in my heart that God sent her. I have no idea what Lorraine said to the management or the owners or whoever it was who had to give the okay. What I do know is that God was working on my behalf. With the stigma of domestic violence I may not have been accepted into the apartment, but, God was in control. I was at a turning point in my life. God found unmerited favor with me, and His mercy is everlasting. I give Him all the glory.

I remember the day I moved in my apartment. I had only my Bible, a sleeping bag, and a picture of my daughter. I remember how happy and free I felt. I danced and praised the Lord. This was the first time I had ever lived on my own alone. There would be tests. I was advancing at my job, which was good. With that came a higher salary. I continued to serve at my church. My banking experience helped me become a trustee at my church. I got involved in ministry at the military base. I had best friends who had been so supportive of me. Now I had the opportunity to decide what I was going to do with the rest of my life. I still suffered from low self-esteem and insecurities. I was still hiding the pain of many years of abuse and rejection. I was still escaping from it all by smoking marijuana in my downtime. Marijuana helped me relax and forget. I never thought I was doing anything wrong. Smoking marijuana was so common in those days. My girlfriends would come over, and we would smoke and talk. It was a social thing, something we shared when we got together. I never thought about how God viewed it. There were numerous tests and trials. I failed some, and some I passed with unwavering faith. There was a struggle going on inside of me between wanting to serve God wholeheartedly and letting go of the secular world. I was still giving in to desires of my flesh. I was seeking joy, peace, and happiness in all the wrong things because I was walking in ignorance. I was learning about God and Jesus, but I still lacked the understanding. I had not yet learned about spiritual warfare. I could feel a change coming over me because many of the things of the world no longer enamored me. I no longer enjoyed doing the things I used to see as fun. With all God had shown me, I remained unsettled in my spirit. I knew something was wrong. When I wasn't at work, I would want to get away from people and be alone with my thoughts. This was not depression. I wanted change. I no longer wanted to live the secular life. I wanted to live the life I had been reading about in my Bible, but I did not know how. I knew it had to be more to it than going to church. My prayer life had decreased. I was not satisfied with that. Prayer had helped free me and save my life. Even though God had delivered me from the hands of the enemy, I still struggled in my faith. I had a lot of distractions that I felt kept me from truly knowing who I was and what God's real purpose was for me in this life. There was a desire in me to do what was right and to tell people about my godly experience. But how could I tell my friends and the people I knew about Jesus and my encounter with the Holy Spirit without anyone thinking I was having a breakdown. It seemed to me that everyone went to church, but they very rarely talked about God after church. I was perplexed. I wanted more. With what I had witnessed, I knew there was more to this faith walk, and I wanted to know more about it. I was hungry for righteousness. I wanted more than just to read the Word of God. I wanted it to come alive to me. If I was going to live out the Word of God, I wanted the understanding. So far I felt as if I had been skimming the surface. I had a Holy Ghost experience, and I wanted to know Him.

I wanted to understand why I would fail in some way every time I wanted to do the right thing and live according to God's standards. I had the desire to do right, but my flesh was not willing. My flesh was at war with my spirit. Thank God I knew to pray. God answered quickly with **Romans 7:14–25**. Paul, the greatest apostle who ever lived, talks about his own struggle with sin. He speaks about how we are human and slaves to sin. These words became real to me and helped bring the understanding I was looking for. I was learning that being born again takes a moment of faith, but becoming like Christ is a lifelong process. Paul got it right when he said there is not a problem with God's law. The law is good and is meant to help us and guide us into God's truth. Paul said the problem is the sin in us that makes us do evil things. Paul admitted to his own failings and confessed that because of his old nature (his nature before Christ), there was no good in him. He confessed that because of his old nature, he was rotten through and through. Paul talks about how he had trouble making himself live right. Paul goes on to talk about his desire to do the right thing. However, every time he tried to do the right thing, evil was always present. Paul anguished over the fact that there was a war going on in his mind that made him a slave to the sin within him. Paul realized that Jesus Christ, our Lord and Savior, was the only answer.

God certainly knows how to answer prayer. He will give you the right words at the right time. When I received this scripture from the Holy Spirit, I knew God was speaking directly to me and helping me understand my own struggle. I was learning that every answer I needed was in God's Word. I was learning to read it and pray for the understanding to come. It doesn't get any clearer than **Romans 7:14–25**. As I came to realize that God was speaking to me through His Word, I wanted to delve into it more deeply. I was hungry for the Word. The Bible states in **Matthew 5:6 (NKJV), "Blessed are they that hunger and thirst for righteousness, for they shall be filled."**

Now that my spiritual eyes had been opened, I could see my sin. I was no longer walking in the ignorance of my sin. The Holy Spirit was working in me and revealing my indiscretions. I actually started feeling guilty that I had sinned greatly against God. I was still struggling between knowing what was right and doing it, and I was also resisting giving into the sins of my fleshly nature. God has made it clear in His Word that we can't serve two masters. He has even made a way of escape. **Romans 8** is all about living life in the Spirit. It is the Holy Spirit who gives us the power we need to live the Christian life. Without Jesus, we would have no hope at all. When Jesus went to the cross, He promised He would come again, but until that time with salvation, we receive the gift of His Holy Spirit, who would come to live in us and guide us into all truth.

God could not have made it any clearer to me. To continue in my sin would bring death. He had made a way of escape for me. I had to make a choice. I was either going to follow Him or my flesh.

I knew God had just spared my life when He delivered me from the hands of my enemy. I no longer wanted to live in fear, and the things of this world didn't appeal to me. I needed God to fix me, to fix everything that was wrong about me. I wanted a do-over. I was so thankful for all God had done, but I was not happy inside. I still suffered the side effects from years of abandonment, abuse, and rejection. Self-destruction and low self-esteem seemed to be my driving force. I did not want these demonic emotions to be my driving force. I was plagued with the guilt of knowing that God had seen my every sin. How could He forgive me? God wanted to restore me, and I knew I needed the restoration. Even more importantly, I wanted it. According to James Robison's narrative on "The Holy Spirit and Restoration" (NKJV), to restore is to bring back to a former or original condition. I believe in this case my restoration would bring me back to the original condition God meant for me when I was in my mother's womb. Outside the womb I had known nothing but rejection, heartache and much pain and suffering. It was hard for me to believe that God had laid out that path for me. Robison states that restoration in every dimension of human experience is at the heart of the Christian gospel. I now know that God had a plan to restore me according to His plan for my life. Robison goes on to state that when something is restored in the scriptures, it is always multiplied or improved so that it's latter state is significantly better than its original state. Robison references **Joel 2:21–26** during a time of restoration and spiritual renewal for the children of Israel. Using Job as an example, Robison reminds us that God multiplies when He restores. Robison reminds us how God restored Job after the terrible trials he endured. He gave him twice what he had lost and blessed him more in his latter days than in the beginning. I could not be restored without repentance and total surrender. God was letting me know I could not come halfway with Him. It was all or nothing. I could not have one foot in the world and the other in the kingdom of God. I could not straddle the fence. I had to come completely and fully surrender myself to Him.

I truly wanted to follow Him, but I needed guidance. I needed to know how to put my faith in action. There was a war going on inside of me, and I needed the kind of help that only God could give.

—m—

Feeling unsettled, I wanted to get away from all the distractions in my life. I needed to get away from all the temptations in my life until I was stronger or mature enough in my Christian walk to take authority over them myself. In His Word, God has promised that we would have authority over temptations, but without being in right relationship with Him, we are powerless. I had so much to learn. I am reminded about temptation in **1 Corinthians 10:13**. The Word of God says, He will not tempt us beyond what we can tolerate, and He tells us He will pave a way of escape for us.

We are called to recognize people and situations that give us trouble and to run from anything we know is wrong. God gives us a choice and asks us to choose to do only what is right. God wants us to pray for His help and to seek fellowship with friends who love God and can offer help when we are tempted. The first step to being set free and gaining the victory is in running from tempting situations.

Feeling the need to get away, I went to the Lord in prayer. Spiritually, I was growing. I had learned the importance of prayer. I was no longer running from situations. I was running to God. I started researching places to live. I had been working for eleven years at the naval base, and I enjoyed the work I was doing; however, I felt there was more that God had for me, and I wanted to find out what that was even if it meant leaving the base. My boss was saddened when I told her. She valued me as an employee, but she gave me her blessing. God answered my prayer, and I moved to New Orleans. This was yet another turning point in my life.

When the plane touched down in New Orleans, I got a feeling that I had made a mistake. I immediately felt that this was not going to be a permanent move. My gut was telling me I would be moving back home. I did not know when, but I knew I would not be staying in New Orleans forever. I was so sure that I didn't even throw out my moving boxes. I never even opened all of them. I stacked them in my storage closet, prepared for my move back home.

The culture was different. Witchcraft and voodoo were acceptable religions in New Orleans. I would soon learn that such practices along with astrology were sins against God.

I lived in New Orleans for two and a half years, and during my time there, God began His cleaning out and restoration process on me. I was totally alone. I had no family or friends there, and I came to depend wholly on God. He had allowed me to move away from all the distractions in my life, and now God had my undivided attention. I used to pray that God would change me from the inside out. I asked Him to purge me of all the hurt and emotional pain that had kept me from reaching my fullest potential in Him. I ask for God to forgive me for my sinful living and to purge me of every unclean thing that would result in sin against Him and His plan for my life.

I read **Psalm 51**. It is a prayer of confession and repentance. David had sinned greatly against God, and he was desperately seeking God's mercy, forgiveness, and cleansing. He poured his heart out before the Lord, and he was truly sorry for his sins against God when he committed adultery and murder. Psalm 51 is my favorite Psalm because it shows David's true love and reverence for the Lord. David truly expresses one of the clearest examples of repentance in all of Scripture.

> **"Have mercy upon me, O God according to thy loving kindness: according unto the multitude of they tender mercies blot out my transgressions. Wash me thoroughly from my guilt, and cleanse me from my sin. For I acknowledge my transgressions: and my sin is ever before me. Against you and you alone, have I sinned and done this evil in thy sight: that you might be justified when you speak, and be clear when you judge. I was born a sinner from the moment my mother conceived me. You desire truth in the inward parts and in the hidden part you make me to know wisdom. Purify me from my sin and I will be clean, wash me and I will be whiter than snow. Make me to know joy and gladness again, now that you have broken me, let me rejoice. Don't keep looking at my sins. Remove the stain of my guilt".**

David goes on to ask God to create in him a clean heart and to renew the right spirit within him. David also asks that God not banish him or take the Holy Spirit from him. He requests that God restore to him the joy of his salvation. He promises to teach sinners about God's ways so they, too, will return to God. David recognizes that God wants a repentant spirit and a contrite heart. David promises to sing of the Lord's forgiveness and to praise Him. David's prayer helped me examine my own heart.

David was a great king. He was known as "a man after God's own heart," but David was not without his own sin. As I've said before, we Christians are not infallible. David had committed the sin of adultery and murder. David's sins affected many people. David repented of those sins and pleaded with God for mercy, forgiveness, and cleansing. He poured his heart out with repentance before God. He let God know that He was serious. Like David, we need to do the same if we want to draw closer to God. We cannot let sin continue to be a barrier between us and God.

God does not want any of us to perish. God is offering us full and complete lives, but the sin in our lives keeps us from drawing close to Him. And unless we confess those sins, intimacy is impossible. This does not mean there will not be consequences for our sins, but God will restore our relationship to Him and will restore our joy. For those believers who have fallen into the sinful ways of the world, know that God is calling you back to Him. He reveals Himself to us in many ways. He does not always do so in a powerful and overt way. Many times if we listen, we can hear Him in the quiet of a humbled heart. His words may come in a gentle whisper. In those quiet moments when we shut out the noise of the world around us and shut off our thinking, we will hear Him speak to us.

I wanted this type of forgiveness. When God opens your spiritual eyes to all your sins, you will feel the shame and guilt that comes with it. It should make you want to repent. He is an all-seeing, all-knowing God. Everything we do, He sees. It's like being naked, and most of us do not want to be seen without any clothes on. Our immediate response to our nakedness is to cover up (much like Adam and Eve). When God opens our spiritual eyes to our sins, our sins become our nakedness, and our covering is repentance. Before our spiritual eyes can be opened we have to be in a right relationship with God. Being in a right relationship means receiving the gift of salvation through the blood of our Lord and Savior, Jesus Christ, by accepting Him through confession and walking in the statutes established in the Word of God. God knows that we will falter. Christians are not infallible. We are just saved. True repentance and turning from our sins brings God's forgiveness into our lives.

I was able to acquire a job working for the military in New Orleans. God found favor with me and made it an easy transition into my new job. I started looking for a church. I asked a few of my coworkers who were Christians where they worshipped. I was invited to several churches. I visited those churches, but I was not enamored. Another coworker told me about Greater St. Stephen's Full Gospel Baptist Church near where I lived. She felt it would be a good fit for me. She said that it was a large church and that the Word there was powerful. I prayed about it and asked God to help me find a church where I could grow. A couple weeks later, I received a call from my sister in Pennsylvania. She informed me that someone at her church in Philadelphia told her to tell me to visit the Greater St. Stephen's Church in East New Orleans. I knew then that God was confirming my prayer. (I had never spoken with my sister about the matter.) I knew that God was confirming that Greater St Stephen's Full Gospel Baptist Church would become my new church home. I was getting used to going to God in prayer and getting confirmation. I truly did not want to repeat the mistakes of my past. I was able to discern in my heart that this was the church God wanted me to be a part of. God used my sister to confirm what was already in my spirit.

I attended worship services and Bible studies. I was hungry to learn. I learned a lot about my spiritual walk. I was never confident in my ability to pray in a group setting. I prayed God would help me in this area. This church was different from the Baptist churches I had been a part of in the past. Though I was raised Baptist, this church was like none I had seen. They celebrated God in their worship. They loudly lifted up the name of Jesus and gave praise to Him. I couldn't tell if it was Baptist or Pentecostal. There were drums and instruments, and Bishop Paul Morton was a singing pastor with a powerful anointed voice. The Word was powerful and reached to the very essence of my soul. This pastor did not mince words. He told it like it was with powerful biblical truths. He preached the Bible. I felt so free in my worship. I could shout hallelujah, and no one would look at me funny because we were all shouting and celebrating the Lord. It was new to me, and it was uplifting. I was in a Bible-teaching, Bible-believing, Holy Ghost-filled church, and I loved it.

It was here I learned about deliverance. There were still some things in my life that I needed to be delivered from. I would come to know that those things were sins against God. I was still reading astrology books and doing astrological charts for people. All of this falls under the sin of witchcraft. There are some things we engage in that we see as harmless in our human ignorance. Astrology is one of those practices that God says falls under witchcraft, which is an abomination to His name. I would come to find out that God's law explicitly forbids these practices in **Leviticus 19:26 and 19:31**, and these activities are also listed among others in **Galatians 5:16–21**.

The desires of our sinful nature include idolatry, sorcery (astrology, mediums, fortune-tellers, etc.), hostility, quarreling, jealousy, outbursts of anger, selfish ambition, dissension, division, envy, drunkenness, sexual immorality, impure thoughts, eagerness for lustful pleasure, wild parties, participation in demonic activities, the feeling that everyone is wrong except those in your own little group, and other sins like these. God has made it clear that those who belong to Christ Jesus have nailed the passions and desires of our flesh to His cross and crucified them.

God could not have made it any clearer. Throughout the Bible, God's Word references these sins. I was still walking in ignorance, trying to get right before the Lord. I did not know that some things were so ingrained in my psyche that only the Holy Spirit could deliver me from them. It all seemed so innocent to me. I never thought that doing astrological charts was introducing evil spirits into my life. No wonder I had such a restless spirit. It was like trying to walk with the Lord and the devil at the same time.

God knew I was walking in ignorance. He had mercy on me and saw to it that I would learn how I was sinning against Him.

One day while I was lying on my living room floor in New Orleans, working on an astrological chart for one of my coworkers (who was not saved), I felt a dark spirit come upon me. I could not move. I sat on the floor in a daze. A sadness came over me. I started feeling depressed. I had not had this feeling since the Lord had saved my life and delivered me from the hands of my enemy on May 31, 1987. I had a prayer partner and sister in Christ who used to give me a ride to work. She called, but I did not answer the phone. I just sat on the floor in front of my astrology books, staring at them. I could not finish the chart I was working on. My prayer partner and Christian friend came to my house because she was worried about me. When she called out, I was able to get up and open the door. She expressed her concerns and noticed the books and charts on the floor. She quickly told me that what I was doing was an abomination against God. She told me that the Holy Spirit was grieved by what I was doing and that I needed to get this stuff out of my home. I now understood where the darkness was coming from. My prayer partner and I swept the house and removed every book and all related materials from my home. We took them into the back woods in Louisiana and burned them in a wire basket. We prayed as they burned. We made sure all of them had burned and then doused them with water. I did not want to be responsible for anyone else finding this material, reading it, and possibly keeping it, causing them to stumble. God holds us responsible if we allow our sins to cause someone else to stumble.

I reflect on the time my daughter called me and bragged to me about how good she was getting at doing astrology charts. She proudly boasted, "I'm almost as good as you, Mom." I panicked briefly as I realize that I myself had handed down this sinful practice to my daughter just as my grandmother had handed it down to me. Did I want my daughter going to hell? She was innocent. She had learned this activity by watching me. I had never sat her down and taught her about astrology and how to do charts, but children are smart. They are like sponges. They absorb everything we do and say. I knew I had to immediately correct this. I told her to stop and get rid of all her astrology books and anything connected to the practice. I admitted to my daughter that I was wrong in practicing astrology, and I told her that it was an abomination against God. As I was coming to learn the error of my ways, I wanted to help keep her from stumbling. I repented to God and asked His forgiveness for teaching my daughter about astrology and psychics. I found out that she had also been frequenting fortune-tellers and psychics while away at school. It was imperative that I tell her God's truth about these practices. I was so happy that she listened to me. She did not argue any point. She just listened. I talked about God and how He viewed these practices. I told her how God detested such practices. Although she had been saved at the age of sixteen, I knew that she had not gotten the teachings that I was now receiving. She was away at college, and I doubt that she was even going to church at that time. I started sending her Christian literature, and I also shipped her a Bible. When I would talk with her on the phone, I would minister to her about the Lord. She never argued with me or debated the issue. She was receptive to what she heard. I wanted to see her in heaven, not hell. The Bible tells us that if we raise our kids on the right path, they will not leave it when they get older.

I would rather teach someone about the Lord and how to get into heaven than help them fall into sin and go to hell. I never argued with my prayer partners when they advised me. I knew they were mature in the Word of God and that they knew God's

Word so much better than I did. Even though I had been saved since the age of thirteen, I was like a babe in Christ. I had not been following the Word of God, and I had not been walking in His statutes or obeying His commands. I was just saved. I had God's grace and mercy covering me, but I did not know Him then. I was seeking to know more about God and why He had saved me from death. I did not deserve His grace and mercy. It was unmerited. I knew through the years that God had used various people to show me the way, and not all of them had been Christians. Looking back, I feel God sent them to me to help me toward fulfilling His ultimate purpose and will for my life. You must remember I was seeking God's will for my life, so it was easy to listen to those who knew the Lord and were walking in a right relationship with Him. I was hungry, and God was feeding me. I wanted God to work through me the way I had witnessed Him working through others who were in a right relationship with Him. I knew that even as a Christian, I could fail. God had saved my life many times. I knew I should have been dead, but His grace and mercy through the blood of Jesus Christ carried me through.

I started going to deliverance services at my church in New Orleans. I did not know what to expect. One time during an altar call, I felt the urging of the Holy Spirit tell me to get up to receive my deliverance and my healing. I had never experienced this kind of worship before. It was all new to me, but I wanted them to lay their hands on me. I knew I needed spiritual and emotional healing. I also knew I needed deliverance from my past, which had been haunting me. I was obedient to the stirring in my heart, although I did not know what to expect. I witnessed people falling out on the floor, and there was a wave of what I called holy emotions flowing across the church. I wanted God to do whatever He needed to do to get me where He needed me to be, and I did not want to be hindered by anything. I wanted deliverance from all the hurt and pain I had been silently carrying around while pretending everything was okay. I could still feel the stinging remnant of abandonment, rape, physical and emotional abuse, rejection, and fear of failure, not to mention the spirit of generational witchcraft that had been leading my life into the cesspool of self-destruction. These were hindrances to my walk with the Lord, and I wanted to be free of them. I was truly a lost soul seeking my God through the power of the blood of Jesus Christ, in whom I put my trust. I went up to the altar for the laying on of hands. Afterward, I immediately started speaking in tongues. God was doing a new thing in me, and I was open to it. I remember sitting there one evening, worshipping God, and praying for all those who were receiving their deliverance. I remember thinking to myself how I wanted to be delivered from the spirit of witchcraft that had governed my life for so long. Witchcraft covers a wide field. A lot of people think that it is all about witches and goblins, but I've got news for you. The sin of witchcraft covers a variety of sins—idolatry, astrology, numerology, psychics, mediums, fortune-tellers, presumptions, stubbornness, sorcery, wizards, enchantments, black magic, jealousy, fits of rage, dissensions, sexual immorality, sensualities, divinations, rebellion, séances, seductions, Ouija boards, illicit drugs, Eastern meditation, and palmistry to name a few. Any practice that dabbles in a power source other than the Lord Jesus Christ is witchcraft. We leave ourselves wide open to Satan when we engage in these practices. That open door can wreak havoc on our lives without our knowing it. God makes it very clear in His Word that these things are forbidden. I never gave any thought to these activities before because it was something I had learned at home. My grandmother read astrology and went to psychics and fortune-tellers. It all seemed so innocent, but now I was learning that many of the things that are acceptable to the world are unacceptable to God. In fact, they are abominations to Him. I was trying to draw close to God, not repel Him. I wanted to get rid of anything that was hindering, anything God may have wanted to do through me. I had come to know that only He could help me in this area. I had been walking in total ignorance of God, but now He was removing the spiritual blinders from my eyes. He speaks clearly through His Word about what is acceptable and what is not. In the books of Deuteronomy, Leviticus, Exodus, 2 Kings, and Acts, we are instructed not to participate in these kinds of behaviors. Once this fact was pointed out to me and I read it for myself, I knew I needed to repent of these sins and receive my deliverance from them so that they would no longer have an influence over my life.

I remember one time while sitting at a deliverance service and praying for others who had responded to the altar call, I listened to all of the sins that people were calling out. I sat there and thought to myself, *they did not call the sin of witchcraft.* I remember saying to the Lord, "I want to be free of this spirit of witchcraft that has governed my life for so long." I told the Lord I wanted to confess and repent for myself and family members who had dabbled in these familiar practices. Then I heard the pastor invite anyone who wanted to receive deliverance from the spirit of witchcraft. I immediately got up and went to the altar. The pastor laid hands on me and prayed a powerful prayer. I knew I had received my forgiveness and deliverance. I remember feeling so free. The Lord was faithful, and I was free to follow Him. I went home in a continued state of praise, rejoicing in His faithfulness. I was reminded **of Psalm 23** and how the Lord was restoring my soul, leading me on the path of righteousness. I was reminded how God walked with me through the valley of the shadow of death. I truly felt the joy of the Lord.

I was learning that a true relationship with God involved more than just going to church on Sunday. I wanted to know more about God's truths. You have to have a true desire for change in your life, and you have to be open to allow God to bring about those changes no matter what. I was at that point. I wanted to know Him. I knew that doing things my way and living for me was not going to do it. I began wanting to live for God. I was saved. (With salvation comes unmerited grace and mercy.). I knew it was God's will that I was still alive. I wanted everyone to know this wonderful sovereign God I had come to know. I wanted them to know what He had done for me and how He had saved my life. God had come through for me, and I was eternally grateful. My spiritual eyes were open. I hold to the promise in 2 **Timothy 4:18 (NKJV)**, which says, **"And the Lord will deliver me from every evil work and preserve me for His heavenly kingdom. To Him be glory for ever and ever. Amen!"** I was ever ashamed before Him as I thought about all the things I had done both knowingly and unknowingly. I humbly confessed each and every sin and asked God for forgiveness. Confession is good for the soul. I felt unworthy to be in His presence. In my spiritual growth, I have come to realize that this is a normal feeling when we come to really know the Lord. When the blinders are removed, we realize what sinful wretches we have been. We are just like our ancestors Adam and Eve. When God opened their eyes to their sin, they were immediately ashamed, and they hid. Hiding is not something God wants us to do. He would rather we come to Him and confess our sins. Christian World Ministries addressed this very thing in *The Feeling of Unworthiness in His Presence*. They say,

> Sometimes we realize God's awesomeness and we feel unworthy to be in His Presence or to go to Him, due to His true love and character. The truth is that when we become His dear children through Jesus Christ, we are made worthy and restored to Him. God desires us to do more than just ask Jesus Christ into our heart and become converted. We are to continue in an ongoing relationship with Him. Even in maintaining our relationship

with Him, He knows that we need His help and He is faithful to us by supplying it.

They go on to teach the following:

> This is not a come to Him one time deal. He desires for us to grow closer to Him, getting to know Him through an ongoing and continuous basis. As we mature and grow in Him many things in our lives will be seen for what they really are. Remember God already knew that those things were in your life before you chose to give your life to Him. Our Heavenly Father wants to reveal things to us so that we can see the lies that we have been told and believe. He wants us to be set free in areas of our lives where we are deceived (believe a lie and think that we are okay). In other words, we come to Him and exchange whatever darkness is for the Truth and receive a fresh new way of thinking and living causing you and me to be changed, therefore coming closer to Him. He has taken the first step! It is up to us to respond by taking the next step by accepting the gift of Eternal Life through Jesus Christ.

I believe we are all by-products of the choices we make in life, whether good or bad. In Christ, we all have been delivered from someone, someplace, or something. Some extreme cases require deliverance from all three (like me).

One day when I was reading about Jesus's crucifixion in my Bible, I cried before the Lord. I had read this story many times before, but it had never had that effect on me before. Now that my eyes were wide open and I was in a true relationship with my God, I came to realize just how much God loved me and just how much He sacrificed for me. As I began to truly realize the magnitude of Jesus's suffering, I cried harder. I was sitting on the floor of my living room with tears streaming down my face, and I looked up and cried out, "You did this for me." I could feel the warmth of the Holy Spirit comforting me as I cried. I knew I could never go back to the life God delivered me from. I knew that God had a hold on me and that my life was forever changed. I was free from the feelings of abandonment, rejection, abuse, depression, pain and suffering, low self-esteem, confusion, anxiety, stress, destructive sins of omission and commission, lustful pleasures, adultery, idolatry, astrology, fortune-telling, psychics, hostility, jealousy, outbursts of anger, drugs, drunkenness, partying, revelry, fornication, and any other desire originating from our sinful nature. I knew that my sanctification was going to be a process, and I was ready. I wanted to live a changed life for Christ.

I started praying and fasting regularly. My prayer partner, who was rooted and grounded in the Word of God, and I would get together weekly and pray. We prayed about everything and everyone the Holy Spirit brought to our hearts. I wanted God to know that I was serious about my walk with Him. I knew God was real and that He exists just as Satan exists. If you don't believe there is a devil, just try doing the right thing. Try living right for God. Satan only attacks those who are trying to live right lives for God. Job is a good example. Satan does not attack those who are already doing his bidding. He doesn't need to. I never felt his attacks until God opened my eyes to my sinful life and my suffering. Up until that point, I had accepted my struggle and my abuse as my norm. It was just my lot in life. I soon found out how wrong I was. I was learning that I did not have to accept what the enemy was handing out. I first had to learn about the choices I had available. I had to learn about God and how He worked through the blood of Jesus

Christ. I had to learn about His love for me. I had to learn who I was in Christ, who had already paved the way of escape for me. I had to learn about the importance of prayer and the importance of reading my Bible daily. God had not hidden anything from me. I just needed a desire to know Him, and He provided that for me through my trials and tribulations, which led to my pain and suffering and brought me to my knees in all humility. If it were not for His salvation through Jesus Christ, whom I accepted as my personal Lord and Savior at the age of thirteen, I would be dead, crazy, or in prison. I found unmerited favor with God because of Jesus Christ, our sacrificial Lamb. He died so that I could be set free from the penalty of sin, hell, death, and the grave. God was faithful and kept His promises. He heard my cry and delivered me. I no longer walk in fear of what man could do to me.

Isaiah 35:4–10 encourages us to be strong and not fear. Isaiah reminds us that God will save us and destroy our enemies. Isaiah gives us a message of hope in verse 10. It depicts the joy of the redeemed. The redeemed are those who have repented of their sins, turned away from them, and accepted Jesus Christ as their personal Lord and Savior.

"Our lives can sometimes become barren and non-productive. We can be overcome with difficulties and trials that can hamper our happiness and security, but God with His marvelous grace (unmerited favor) can bring fresh meaning to fruitless and discouraged lives. He does it however, according to our willingness to be instruments of His redemptive purpose for the world. God intends good for all of us, and He intends to secure it through Jesus Christ. Christians are to be ambassadors for the kingdom of God. It is our responsibility to be involved in Jesus' concerns for healing, for the poor, and those people society ignores".

I was one of those people who was living a fruitless and

discouraged life. Through confession, repentance and renewing my covenant with the Lord, God forgave me, delivered me, and restored to me the joy of His salvation. He put my feet on the straight and narrow path.

God was starting to do a good work in me. I was seeking Him more. I thirsted for His Word. I was learning about the power of prayer, and I wanted to walk in His truth. I wanted to know His will for my life. I also wanted others to know this amazing God who had saved me from the throes of death and brought change and stability to my life. I wanted everyone I knew to know that God, Jesus, and the Holy Spirit are real. I stood on the promises of God, and I trusted in Him. I witnessed the power of the Holy Spirit. Would people think I was crazy if I told them about this truth? I did not care. I knew I had to minister so that others would come to believe and know that God is real. God was truly at work in me, and I had no doubt He was calling me into ministry. I was going to be a living witness for the Lord.

My prayer partner and I started taking prayer walks in various neighborhoods in New Orleans. We would stop in front of vacant buildings and pray. We laid hands on the doors and windows, asking God to breathe new life into these businesses. The Holy Spirit would stop us in front of houses and urge us to pray for these homes. We would use our gift of speaking in tongues as directed by the Holy Spirit. God was using me and moving in ways I would have never thought possible. I was obedient to His Holy Spirit. I knew I needed to be careful because Satan was angry and seeking to destroy me. God expects us to take an assertive stance against the devil and his evil works. He has given us the power through the blood of Jesus Christ to take authority over any situation the devil may try to use against us. We must be spiritually alert and fully clothed in our spiritual armor to oppose any attacks from Satan. We are reminded of this in Ephesians.

> **Finally my brethren, be strong in the Lord and in the power of His might. Put on the whole armor of God that you may be able to stand against the wiles of the devil. For we do not wrestle against flesh and blood, but against principalities, against powers, against the rulers of the darkness of this age, against spiritual hosts of wickedness in heavenly places. Therefore take up the whole armor of God that you may be able to withstand in that evil day, and having done all to stand. Stand therefore having girded your waist with truth, having put on the breastplate of righteousness, and having shod your feet with the preparation of the gospel of peace; above all take the shield of faith with which you will be able to quench all the fiery darts of the wicked one. And take the helmet of salvation and the sword of the spirit, which is the word of God; praying with all prayer and supplication in the Spirit being watchful to this end with all perseverance and supplication for all the saints-and for me, that utterance may be given to me that I may open my mouth boldly to make known the mystery of the gospel for which I am an ambassador in chains, that I may speak boldly as I ought to speak. (Ephesians 6:10–19 NKJV)**

I got a lesson in this firsthand. One evening after attending a weekday worship service at my church, I went home rejoicing in the Lord, giving thanks to Him, and just glorifying Him verbally. I went upstairs to get ready for bed. In the process, the Holy Spirit came over me, and I started leaping for joy in praise to the Lord. It may be impossible for some of you to understand the extent of my newfound appreciation of the Lord God almighty, but if you had survived what I had survived and come through what I had come through with the help of the Lord Jesus Christ through the power of His Holy Spirit, you would understand. If you had walked where I had walked and experienced the same danger, the abuse, and the violence, you would understand the feeling of being delivered and now living a life free from the bondage of your past sins. Many of the people I knew did not make it. God spared me for a reason, and I am here to proclaim His name.

As I leaped for joy, I was passing by one of the floor-to-ceiling windows in my townhouse. I heard a voice clearly say, "jump out the window". Discernment kicked in, and I immediately recognized that it was the voice of Satan. I realized at that point that Satan was still trying to kill me. He was still angry with me for turning from my worldly ways and deciding to live for Jesus Christ. I rebuked Him, put Him out of my house, and commanded him to take his little imps with him. Now some of you may think that that's drastic approach to something I could not see. You might even think it's a little crazy. Well, when many people land in jail or end up dying, they often proclaim, "The devil made me do it." Or they say, "God spoke to me and told me to do it." Satan is deceiving many people who lack a personal relationship with the Lord. (They don't know Him). Therefore, these people lack discernment. You'd better be able to discern when God is talking to you and when Satan is talking to you. The Word of God reminds us that Jesus Christ is the Shepherd of the sheep (us) and that His sheep know His voice.

Most assuredly I say to you, he who does not enter the sheepfold by the door, but climbs up

**some other way, the same is a thief and a robber.
But he who enters by the door is the Shepherd
of the sheep. To him the doorkeeper opens, and
the sheep hear His voice; and He calls His own
sheep by name and leads them out. And when
He brings out His own sheep He goes before
them, and the sheep follow Him for they know
His voice. (John 10:1–4 NKJV)**

—m—

As I continued to grow in my walk, I wanted to share what I
was learning about God and His marvelous works and to share
how He was working in my life. I wanted people to know Jesus the
way I was coming to know Him. I started sending out Christian
evangelism tracts and freely sending Bibles and Christian literature
to people I knew. I shared a lot of what I was learning with my
daughter. I wanted her to know the Lord for herself beyond just
being saved. I wanted her to know where her help came from and
who she could turn to when trials came her way. I wanted her to
know that God was not just a punishing God but a God of love
and compassion. I wanted to break the generational curse that
had been handed down for four generations because of the sins
of our grandparents and parents. I knew there were things they
were doing that laid the groundwork for the next generation. We
had fallen into the same trap set by Satan, who had been using
our trials and tribulations against us to keep us in bondage to
sin. I am reminded that some members of my family fell into
some sinful practices that were an abomination against God, not
unlike the children of Israel. It's easy to see that even Christians
can fall. The main thing I remember about my family teaching
us young ones about God was that He was going to punish us if
we did not do this or that. I was afraid of God and ashamed of

who I was because of the legacy set forth by my family. They had convinced my sister and me that we were the lowest of the low in the family. We were never treated like other family members. We were treated like servants. My self-esteem was destroyed until I learned about God's wonderful redeeming grace. I was on my way to total self-destruction when He took this servant's heart and brought restoration to it. Now He is using it for my good and His glory. I love the Lord. He heard my cry and delivered me.

I was still living in New Orleans when I received a call from my sister in Philadelphia. She told me that my nephew (her son) had tried to commit suicide by stabbing himself in the stomach. She said that he had undergone two surgeries and that he was expecting to receive a third surgery. I started praying immediately for his healing. I felt it imperative that I go home to visit him. I felt it in my spirit that God was going to heal him, but I felt there was something else God wanted me to do. I was open and receptive to whatever God wanted to do. I was usable. God had saved me and brought great change into my life. I had promised Him I would serve Him for the rest of my life. I told a few coworkers in New Orleans that I had to go home and that I was on a mission for the Lord. I wasn't sure how I was going to do it because funds were tight. I knew trying to book a train on short notice would cost more. I prayed about it. I was talking on the phone with my best friend who lived in Philadelphia. I told him about my nephew's suicide attempt and my difficulty getting home to see him. My friend told me that he had just found a check that he had never cashed stuck between the pages of his Bible. He said that it was for $450.00 and that he had no real need for the money. Then he offered to send it to me. In **Philippians 4:19**, God promises that He will supply our every need according to His riches in glory, and this was just another example of His faithfulness. I know without a doubt that God so preserved that check for me. He knew I was going to need money to get home, and He prepared in advance. No one can convince me otherwise because I know that my father in heaven moves in mysterious ways. I had witnessed for myself His marvelous works and was the beneficiary of those works. I knew He was now moving in my life to fulfill His purpose. I doubted nothing. When the money arrived, I took a train home immediately. I went straight to the hospital. Upon entering my nephew's hospital room, I could immediately feel familiar spirits (depression and sickness) in his room. My nephew was a young man, and they had put him in a room with an elderly ailing man who was wailing. I was told this elderly man wailed all night. My nephew had tubes everywhere. He had a lost look in his eyes. I stood back and quietly observed for a few minutes, and as I talked with my nephew and my sister, I heard the voice of the Lord say, "get up and pray." I never questioned why He didn't call my sister, who was the minister, to pray. Although normally shy about praying in front of others, I was obedient. The Spirit of the Lord was upon me, and I could feel Him. I never thought I could pray as well as some people like ministers and deacons, but I knew God would answer even an imperfect prayer. While I was in the room, God revealed to me that my nephew's healing was already in progress. God called me to pray with him and lay hands on him as there was still a spirit of hopelessness and depression that had caused him to try to commit suicide in the first place.

I took my nephew's hand and ask that the rest of the family in the room join me by holding hands. A powerful prayer went forth, and as I prayed, I could feel an energy pass from my hand to my nephew's. I knew he felt it because his grip tightened. I returned to New Orleans the next day (Sunday). On Monday I received a call from my nephew. He sounded strong and elated. He called to thank me for making the long trip to pray with him. He told me that after I left, they changed his room. (I did not request that. It was God's doing.) He went on to state that his bowels were working once again and that he had eaten his first meal. He also stated that the nurses had taken down his IVs, and the doctors told him that he would be discharged from the hospital on Wednesday of that week. He stated they told him that he would no longer need any more surgeries. He stated, "It wasn't until you came and prayed for me that things got better, and I just want to thank you."

I said, "Praise the Lord," and then I advised him to thank God because I had nothing to do with his healing. I again told him to thank the Lord. I knew I was just a vessel God used, and I was not going to steal His glory by taking the credit for anything other than being a willing and obedient servant. I know that God could have healed my nephew without me being there. As a matter of fact, his physical healing had already begun long before I got there. It just had not manifested yet. When I prayed and laid hands on my nephew, it was completed. The spirit of depression that made him attempt suicide was defeated. What a wonderful testimony of God's divine healing. I always felt that God called me to go to Philadelphia because there was something He wanted me to learn. I believe He was testing my obedience.

By faith, I believe in the laying of hands. I had received my own deliverance from the spirits of depression, rejection, abuse, and carnality through the laying of hands of the saints of God. Throughout Jesus's ministry, He laid hands on the sick and healed them. He has promised we would perform miraculous works in His name. I believed it then, and I still believe it now. "And these signs shall follow them that believe; in my name they shall cast out devils; they shall speak with new tongues; they shall take up serpents; and if they drink any deadly thing it shall not hurt them; they shall lay hands on the sick, and they shall recover" (**Mark16:17–18 KJV**).

The following Sunday I gave my testimony before our

congregation about God's awesome healing powers. I wanted to give God the glory He deserved, and I wanted others to know that God can and will heal. He had healed me. After giving testimony about my experience with God, the Holy Spirit fell upon me, and I fell to the floor. (It's called being slain in the Spirit.) When I recovered, an elderly lady I did not know approached me and said, "God told me to tell you your calling is healing." I wasn't sure at that time exactly what that entailed as I still considered myself like a newborn baby in Christ. I was still in the learning and discovery phases of my spiritual walk. But I was hungry, and I wanted to learn. One thing I knew was that God would reveal His plan and purpose for my life when He was ready. God had not let me down thus far, and I knew I just needed to continue trusting Him. He brought good Christian people into my life to help teach me, and His Holy Spirit was guiding me. Healing is one of the spiritual gifts, and I consider it a blessing that God would want to use me to help bring healing to lost souls.

I remember when I was twenty-two years old God healed me when someone tried to poison me by putting LSD in my drink. It sent me on a twenty-four-hour trip that almost led me to taking my own life. **Mark 16:18** says "If they drink any deadly thing, it shall not hurt them." I continue to realize just how often God's mercy was truly looking out for me as I was walking in ignorance in the way of the world. My ignorance and self-destructive ways could have taken me out multiple times, but God and His infinite mercy covered me. Although I was saved, I was not at that time in my life walking the straight and narrow path with the Lord. But He decided that I should live. His grace and mercy saved me from certain death after I drank the concoction meant to bring me harm, not to mention the numerous other occasions when I looked death in the eye. Once again, the grace of God, I am still here. Thank God for salvation through the blood of Jesus Christ, our Lord and Savior.

I love the Lord. He heard my cry and delivered me. I was then and am still eternally thankful. I made a promise to God that if He saved me, I would spend the rest of my life serving Him, and I meant it. I wanted a new life in Him. I wanted Him to restore to me the joy of His salvation. I wanted to let go of all the past with all of its pain and suffering. I was starting to feel the love of God, which was stronger and deeper than any other love. The comfort of His Holy Spirit let me know that everything was going to be all right and that more change was yet to come. I would be tested in various areas of my life, but my faith would not fail me as God had brought the understanding of my Christian walk. **"I will exalt you, Lord, for you rescued me. You refused to let my enemies triumph over me. O Lord my God, I cried for help, and you restored my health. You brought me up from the grave, O Lord. You kept me from falling into the pit of death. Sing to the Lord all you Godly ones! Praise his holy name"** (Psalm 30:1–3 NLT).

In reflecting back on my spiritual journey, I can see where He was preparing me for ministry all along. Even this journey to New Orleans, which I thought was my plan, was actually part of His plan. It allowed me to get away from the distractions that kept me from hearing God's voice and from truly knowing Him. I realize that sometimes God needs to get us alone in order to get our undivided attention. God was doing serious repair and restoration work within me. He knew the plans He had for the rest of my life, and He knew what I needed to fulfill His purpose for my life. The best part is that I was not fighting against Him. I wanted change. I wanted to know true happiness. I wanted to know Him. I had never known love before. I had never been told that I was loved by anyone in my family while I was growing up. I never felt that maternal and paternal love that many people are blessed to experience in life. Because of my ignorance in matters of the heart, I often mistook lust for love in my personal relationships, which caused so much drama in my life. It wasn't until I turned my life over to God that I came to know true love. God's love is the greatest love of all. Feeling Him working in my life; seeing how He changed me; seeing how He took the spiritual blinders off my eyes; and understanding how He saved, forgave, and delivered me was enough for me to realized that I was loved. The very fact that God gave up His only begotten Son, Jesus Christ, to die for my redemption tells me just how much He loved me.

Why am I being so candid with all this? Well, I am hopeful that my testimonies can help someone who may be experiencing similar situations or who may be headed down a similar path. Maybe someone is reading this book who does not know the Lord at all. It is not enough to just be saved. You need to develop a personal relationship with God and be in communication with Him regularly through prayer. You need to know who to turn to and who has all power in His hands. He can take a situation that Satan meant to use to do you harm and turn it into something good. You need to know about the only one who can move inside your heart and change it. You need to know about the only one who will give you unconditional love, and with His unmerited grace and mercy, He can restore your broken life. He will strengthen you where you are weak and repair any damage to your broken soul. You must know that it is only through the blood of Jesus Christ that any of this is possible. Jesus paid the price for our freedom. In **John14:6 (NLT)**, Jesus told the disciples, "I am the way the truth and the life. No one can come to the Father except through Me."

As I continue to reflect back on my journey with the Lord and as I realize that God was with me all along, I am so thankful that

He did not let me die in my sin or suffer in my sorrow. God's grace and mercy is everlasting. Accepting Jesus Christ as my personal Lord and Savior is the best thing I ever did in my life. Think about it! ***Personal Lord and Savior!*** What a gift.

When my journey to New Orleans was over, God allowed me to return to Pennsylvania. I was starting to miss my friends and my family. I prayed to God to allow me to go home again. I remember telling God that I did not want to live my life alone and that I did not trust my emotions in finding someone to complete my life. I told God that I wanted to be married and that I wanted Him to help choose my husband. I wanted someone who was saved and walking with the Lord. My relationship with God had become so real that I could ask Him things like that. God wants us to always consult with Him, especially when making important decisions. I was at a stage in my life with the Lord that I could finally say what I wanted in life and actually expect it to happen. I had a newfound confidence in the Lord. I had never known what it was like to have a father in the natural, but I now knew that I had a spiritual father whose love superseded any natural love that could come from man. I now knew how it felt to be truly loved. My heart was no longer aching for fulfillment of Phileo love (natural love and affection). I had found Agape love (godly).

I wasn't sure how or when I was going to go home to Pennsylvania. I was just trusting God. When I landed in New Orleans, I knew that my stay was not going to be permanent. That's why I never got rid of my moving boxes. God had shown me so much of Himself, and had moved in so many ways. I knew all I had to do was ask, believe, and trust in Him.

I started feeling lonely, and missing all that was familiar to me. New Orleans was a whole different experience for me. The culture was different from what I was used to. I missed Pennsylvania, which was my home. I spoke to the Lord about my feelings. Little did I know that He already had a plan in place. If it was God's will that I should stay in New Orleans, then I would have learned to be content, for **Philippians 10:11** says that we should be content in whatever we have; however, I did not feel that I was supposed to stay there. I now knew that God had allowed the move to New Orleans, and that there was a greater purpose for it. God had placed in my heart the desire to get away from all of the distractions in Pennsylvania. He needed one-on-one time with me to deliver me and develop me. Being in New Orleans all alone, I had no one to depend on but God. I wanted to know Him, and I wanted to draw close to Him. The Bible says, "Blessed are they that do hunger and thirst after righteousness for they shall be filled." The Word of God also says, "God blesses those who are the poor in spirit for theirs is the Kingdom of Heaven" (**Matthews 5:3, 10 KJV**).

I was hungry and wanted to learn more about God and what He expected of me, and I knew I needed Him. I was spiritually poor. There is nothing worse than a spiritually poor and broken Christian, but it can happen when you don't know the Lord and are not in fellowship with Him. God was healing and fixing me, and I wanted what He wanted for me. I knew what Jesus had done, when He died to set me free from the penalty of sin, hell, death, and the grave; however, I did not know how to walk in God's truth. I had not been reading my Bible or praying before this time. My life was filled with all sorts of drama and distractions. Now I was free to walk the path God had carved out for me, so going home (back to Pennsylvania) had to be God's will.

One day while working at my desk in New Orleans, I got a phone call from my supervisor at my previous job in Pennsylvania. She said that our comptroller had asked her to call me and see if I wanted to come back home. Before I left for New Orleans, I had been working in the comptroller's office at the naval air base in Pennsylvania. I had established good working relationships in that office. It was a small office, but it was a big job. Only seven of us were in charge of a very large military budget. I was well respected there, and I was considered an exemplary employee. When I moved, my comptroller was devastated, but she gave me her blessing and told me she would hire me back whenever I wanted. Well, now she was calling me to see if I was ready to come home. I knew God laid that on her heart. I had not spoken to my comptroller since I had left Pennsylvania two and a half years earlier. There is no way she would know I wanted to come back home unless God had laid it on her heart. My supervisor also told me that the desk I used to sit at had been empty for a couple months. The person who took my position had left, and even though my old position had been advertised, no one had applied for it. Do you see the picture? Are you getting it? Remember, I had prayed and asked God if I could go home to Pennsylvania. Now what do you think is going on here? "Ask and you will receive" **(Luke 11:9)**. God was paving the way for me to go home again. His purpose for me in New Orleans had been fulfilled, and I was returning home a new person in Christ.

I quickly responded with a yes, and I instantly started preparing for my return. I was working for our Financial Headquarters in New Orleans, so the transfer back to the Naval Air Station in Pennsylvania, was easy. God was in charge and leading the way. If I had not serviced God well by being an exemplary employee, I doubt that they would have gone through what they did to get me back. God moved swiftly, and within two months, I was back in Pennsylvania. When I walked into my old job, everyone was so glad to see me. One of my coworkers said, "There's something different about you. I don't know what it is, but you are different." What a testimony to the Lord. He works in you, and people will notice.

After returning home, I started reflecting on all that God had brought me through and all that He had done for me. I wanted to know why. I wanted to know my purpose. I knew God had a plan, but I wasn't sure what to do with all I had learned. I wanted to tell the world about the love of God and about how I had called on the name of Jesus in my distress and how He had been there for me. I wanted people to know that God, Jesus, and the Holy Spirit were real. I wanted everyone to know Him the way I was getting to know Him. God still had a work to do in me, but I was on my way to living the true Christian life. I knew there would be times when I would fall short, but I also knew how to go to the Lord in prayer, how to repent, and how to ask for forgiveness. I also learned from any mistakes. I did not repeat them. His grace and mercy are far greater than I deserve. In knowing Him, I desire to serve Him and to follow His commands.

Two years after I arrived home, I married my best friend. God allowed it. It was beautiful. Our love is another testimony to the Lord. It is unbelievable how God moved and allowed the two of us to come together in holy matrimony. My husband is a saved man of God, and I am blessed to have someone who loves me unconditionally and respects me. I don't have to ask for his love and respect. He gives these freely. Jim is someone I used to think was too nice for me. As my friend, I was always trying to fix him up with a nice woman. He had been my best platonic friend since 1977. I would have never thought throughout those years that I was looking at my future husband until God revealed the truth to me while I was in New Orleans. If God had told me I was going to remain single, I would have been fine with that, but He didn't. He revealed to me that Jim was going to be the one. I heard Him say his name very clearly, so clear it woke me out of my sleep one night. I have never regretted it. He is the love of my life, just below God and Jesus.

A wise old woman once told me that healing was my gift. I wanted to know how to use that gift. In 1997, four years after my return to Pennsylvania, I decided to leave my job at the naval base and go back to school for nursing. I associated the gift of healing with ministering to the sick. I was sure God wanted me to care for the physically sick. I wanted to be obedient. I wanted to show God I was serious about serving Him. This would be another turning point in my life. God was opening doors, and I was going to walk through them.

The storms of life did not stop just because I was following Christ and living a changed life. After coming back home, my faith was tested several times. First, we found out that my husband had cancer two weeks after we got married. It was a test that really strengthened us both. We prayed and trusted God. My husband had surgery and survived. He did not have to get treatments. The doctors had caught it in the early stages. God's grace and mercy prevailed along with His healing power.

The second test was the unexpected death of my mother. My mom had lived as a homeless person on the streets of Philadelphia for about seven years. We had searched for her many times, but each time there was a siting, she would disappear on us. She had been in and out mental institutions her entire life. When she got out of the hospital, she vowed never to return again, so she disappeared into the streets like so many of the mentally impaired do. After years living on the streets of Philadelphia, she was found by a wonderful charity and homeless advocate group called Project Homes. It was founded by a nun who does wonderful work with the homeless in Philadelphia, getting them off the streets and acclimated back into society.

As soon as we got the call, our immediate family went to see her. She had been living in a shelter, and she was preparing to move into her own place. She was so happy, but not just to see us. She was happy in general. She looked so good and well kept. My mother was a true believer in the Lord Jesus Christ, and it was apparent that He had kept her in perfect peace and had taken very good care of her while she was living on the streets. She said that she had prayed that God would let her see all of her children again, and there we were.

The doctors said my mother was in excellent health. She was soon back on her psych meds and doing well. Project Homes would do more than just bring people in from the street and put them in shelters. They went a step beyond that. Project Homes buys abandon homes from the city and turn them back into residential homes for the homeless. They are really nice homes in nice neighborhoods. My mom shared a home with three other women who had also been homeless. The home was furnished by Project Homes. They even took the women shopping for furniture and let each pick out their own bedroom furnishings. Each woman had her own bedroom, and they collaborated on the living room, dining room, and kitchen furnishing. At that time Project Homes also owned several businesses (restaurants, thrift shops, and consignment stores). These businesses catered to the public but were run by homeless people. Project Homes would train the homeless and then hire them to work in these businesses. They received a salary for their work. This was all done to help them assimilate back into society. They helped the homeless to open bank accounts and taught them how to save money and how manage their accounts. They provided a home health nurse who visited once a month to give them their monthly medications. A van would pick them up and take them to doctor appointments, grocery shopping, and other activities like the movies, bowling, or eating out for dinner. We visited her often. I was so happy to have my mom back, and for the first time, I had a normal mother-daughter relationship. It was also good to function like a family, something none of us had experienced. I enjoyed visiting Mom on the weekends and talking about our travails in life. During these times Mom revealed a lot of truths about her and my father (whom I never knew) as well as her relationships with the rest of the family. She had no hard feelings toward the family members who had treated her so badly in life. When I asked her why, she responded, "Because they are my family." She definitely had lost all trust in them, but she did not hate them. She talked as if she felt sorry for my grandparents, who had both passed at this time. She talked about how my grandmother had been part of the problem in regards to her relationship with my father. Her memories were vivid, and it was apparent she been through a lot of suffering. She told me about how she had been raped and had been afraid to tell anyone. I could relate to that because I, too, had been raped and never told anyone. I know what it's like to hide that kind of pain.

My mom was opening up more than she ever had in her life. I had never known this side of her. Her candidness moved me. I felt so much closer to her. I remember our last conversation together. We were sitting and talking at her dining room table one afternoon when she looked at me. I remember thinking about how beautiful she looked as she told me about her time on the street. Her voice was filled with gratitude as she spoke about the kindness of strangers and how a couple who owned a Chinese restaurant used to put hot Chinese food out the back of their restaurant for her. She spoke of the nice policeman who used to let her stay on the warm vent in Center City. We laughed as she spoke about the ham she had purchased and heated on the vent. She spoke of how people gave her money, and she would go to the church on Green Street and pay her tithe of 10 percent. Then she would go to the Italian market and buy fruits and vegetables and eat them. She told me how much she appreciated the people at the 30th Street train station who would let her wash up in the bathroom and let her stay there all night so she could be warm in the winter. As she spoke, I reflected on how God was looking out for her and providing for her just like He had done for me. At that moment I looked at

Mom, and all the mistakes she had made in her life didn't matter anymore. She was my mom, and I loved her. I had forgiven her. If she had not chosen to bring me into this world, I would not have the life I've lived, and I could not give this testimony about God's unfailing love toward me and my family.

My mother loved the Lord so much that she was often seen as a fanatic. I believe she knew she was troubled in her mind, so she gave God her heart. She talked about how she would kneel in front of the park bench in Fairmount Park and how she would pray for her children. She said that she used to call each one of us out by name and that God would reveal to her how each of us was doing. I knew she spoke the truth when she told me God revealed to her that Nanny (my nickname) was "just a praying" (meaning that I was praying a lot). It was the truth because I was at that time seeking God's will for my life. I had come through some major turning points that only prayer could deliver me from. I now know that I had ridden on the wings of my mother's prayers. Even in the midst of her own hardships, she had the wherewithal to pray for her children, not knowing where they were or what was happening in our lives. That's faith in action.

Sitting with mom on this day was different. She seemed tired as she turned to me and said, "These meds are killing me. I can't do this anymore". I looked at her, and I understood. I knew about psych meds. I had studied them in nursing school. I told her we could talk with the doctor about reducing the dose. I felt a little selfish. I did not want her to stop taking them altogether and relapse and wind up back out on the street. I was enjoying my time in getting to know her. Even though I was in my forties, the little girl in me still wanted her mother. My mom looked me in my eyes and said, "I'm tired. I had a talk with my Father last night." I knew she meant God because her relationship with God was very personal, and she always referred to him as her Father. She said, "I told him I am ready to come home."

I looked at her, and I said, "Now, Mom, you know God is not going to take you until He is ready."

Mom put her hand on her hip, rolled her eyes, turned her head as if to suggest that I didn't know anything, and said, "I'm outta here." A couple weeks later, she had a syncopal episode and wound up in the hospital. Soon after that, she passed away. I was devastated, but I kept my emotions in. How could I be upset knowing that God had answered her pray and that now she had gone on to be with Him? I had wanted her to be there at my nursing school graduation and to see her great-grandchildren. My heart was broken. I was just getting to really know her. It took weeks after her funeral before I broke down, and then a flood of emotions came over me one day as I was hanging a tribute to her on our wall. I remember sliding down the wall to the floor and screaming. My husband knew immediately what was wrong. He said, "You finally got it out." As he held me, I cried. I was so thankful to have him there for me. I never asked God why. The pain of losing the only parent I'd ever known just as we had finally started bonding was the true test of my faith.

The trials kept coming too. On January 19, 1999, eight months after Mom's passing, my husband and I suffered a devastating fire, and we lost everything we owned, except the clothes we had on our back. We lost a very good friend in that fire as well. Our hearts were saddened, but our faith sustained us. We never asked why. We stood and watched the place burn for a little while as I let the fireman know that our friend was inside. Then we went across the street to the post office vestibule, which was open all night, and we prayed. My husband tried to get into her apartment to save her, but the back draft was too strong. She couldn't get out because the fire had started in her apartment. I was sad, but I was also so thankful that I had led her to Christ a few weeks before. The Holy

Spirit had led me to tell this lovely little Jewish lady about Jesus. She accepted Jesus right in her kitchen.

Once again, God moved quickly. We never had a need from day one of the fire. We never had to ask for anything. God had all kind of supports in place for us. People from the Red Cross, our local council person, the mailman, local post office employees, neighbors, coworkers, and the people from the nursing school I attended all responded and gave out of the goodness of their hearts. We had so much in supplies, clothing, and money that we were able to share some of it with a coworker of mine who had suffered a fire several weeks after our fire. When you are in a right relationship with God, He will take care of you. I never let the death of my mother or the fire stop me from moving forward. I was empowered by how God was moving in our lives.

I finished nursing school and went to work at Abington Memorial Hospital in Abington, Pennsylvania. I am ever grateful to God for allowing me to fulfill a childhood dream. It had been a rough journey, but I looked at how far God had brought me, and I praise His holy name.

I worked at Abington Hospital for four years, caring for the sick on the orthopedic med-surg. and the psychiatric units. I loved it. I often prayed with and for my patients. I loved administering to their physical needs. I saw many get well and go home, and I met some who did not make it. Many of my patients were open to conversations about God and His goodness. The hospital is the one place I have found where patients are more receptive to talking about God. It could be that they are facing situations they know only God can help them with. I don't know, but when many of my patients found out I was a Christian, they asked me to pray for them. One of my patients who was scheduled for surgery asked me directly if I was Christian. When I told him I was, he asked,

"Will you pray with me right now?" I stopped immediately, and he and I prayed together. He was much appreciative and filled with thanks. My heart was filled with joy because I knew God was using me.

I was enjoying my new life in Christ, but I couldn't help but feel that something was missing. I prayed about it all. I had come to learn that prayer was the key to getting the answers I needed. I wanted to be sure that I was doing what God wanted me to do. As a child, I had always dreamed of being a nurse, but back then I thought it was out of reach for me. Now I could see that I could be and do anything I wanted in Christ. What I wanted was to be sure that being a nurse was God's plan for me. I kept feeling like something was missing.

I reflect on the day I decided not to go on to be an RN. As an LPN I had achieved much. I was nominated twice for the Nurse Excellence award at Abington Hospital. I was the recipient of that award in 2003. I was driven to give my best in whatever I endeavored, but I still felt that something was missing. I remember while driving through North Philadelphia one day, I was led to the Center for Urban Theological Studies (CUTS). I had heard about it from my older sister, who graduated from there. I was curious about it. I had been taking courses at the local community college since the early 1980s. I had accumulated quite a few credits. While in nursing school for my licensed practical nurse diploma, one of the requirements was to take the prerequisites for the RN program. It was a fully accredited nursing school with high requirements that prepared you for the RN program (University of Pennsylvania's Presbyterian Medical Center School of Practical Nursing). I had completed all of my prerequisites and as an LPN I could easily transition into the RN program, but I wasn't sure that was what God wanted. I had made so many mistakes in my life that I did not want to make any more. It was important to me that I do God's work. I wanted to fulfill His purpose for my life and not my own. It wasn't about making more money or the glory of being an RN. It was about me fulfilling the purpose God had for my life, and I did not feel that it was in nursing, even though I graduated nursing school with honors and was fulfilling something I thought I had always wanted to become. I am sure I disappointed a few family members. I remember my sister telling me that when she told them I graduated from nursing school, they weren't impressed. They wanted to know why I did not go on to the RN program. They did not understand my reasons, and I could not explain it. To be truthful I really didn't care how they felt. Considering what I had come through, I felt I had made it further than anyone in my family thought I would. I was at a stage in life where I could make choices about how I would spend the rest of it, and it was very important to me that I follow God's plan for my life. I was afraid of the unknown, but God gave me courage. I had tread some dangerous territory in my old life and walked much of it without fear, even though I was standing at death's door most of the time, so how could I fail with God as my copilot now? I believe that sometimes you have to lose in order to gain. I was living that out. Now I was giving up being an RN for something I wasn't quite sure about. Things were happening that I did not fully understand, but I did not let it stop me. In Isaiah 55:8–9, God tells us that His thoughts are nothing like our thoughts and that His ways are nothing like our ways. God works in ways that we cannot even imagine.

I never really felt like I was losing because I decided not to go for the RN program. I was just happy that I was able to reach the goal of becoming any nurse. My family believed that my sister and I would never amount to anything. Just becoming a nurse was proof of how wrong they were. God was trying to show me He had more in store for me if I followed Him. God's legacy for me comes out of **Jeremiah 29:11–14 (NLT)**, which says, **"For I know** the plans I have for you," says the Lord. "They are plans for good and not for disaster to give you a future and a hope. In those days when you pray I will listen. If you look wholeheartedly for me, you will find me. I will be found by you says the Lord. "I will end your captivity and restore your fortunes."

For me there was no question. I was going to follow God's plan. I never thought it was going to be easy, but I was going to trust Him. I was encouraged by a God who believed in me and encouraged me through His Word to keep going. He let me know that I was stronger than I knew and that He would be with me all the way. In Jesus Christ, there is nothing that I can't accomplish. God gave me hope. God knows our future, and if we follow Him, He will provide us with what we need to fulfill His purpose for our lives. In Him, there is boundless hope. This does not mean we will be spared pain, suffering, or hardship, but God will see us through to a glorious conclusion as He did with me. I was ready for anything. I knew that it could not be worse than what I had already endured. Jesus was my Advocate, and I was committed to following Him. I still am committed to following Him.

I was taking courses at the Deliverance Evangelistic Bible Institute in Philadelphia. I did well there. I was an "A" student. Between there and community college, I was making grades that I never could have made when I was in junior high and high school. In my younger years, I never took school seriously. School used to be a place where I escaped to get away from the emotional trauma and abuse we received. I never really wanted to learn. I was a troubled young girl, and no one seemed to care. My family always thought I was dumb because I was quiet. They even called me sneaky because I did not talk. They were too dumb to realize how traumatized my sister and I were from all the abuse we had been through. They didn't understand how the loss of our parents could affect me and my sister at such a young age. No one cared enough to ask how we were feeling. They valued our lives less than that of other family members, and they never respected us. Our self-esteem was so low that only God could lift it up.

Now here I was many years later picking up the pieces of my life, and with the help of the Lord, I had survived a volatile childhood without a mother or a father. I had endured foster care, mental/emotional abuse, rape, drugs, domestic abuse, death, the loss of my mother, and a devastating fire, that resulted in the death of a close friend and the loss everything we owned. I have no doubt that God was with me through it all, and that is why I am alive now to tell the story. I could not have made it if He were not working in my life to help me overcome. I was thinking about all this in my mind as I parked my car and approached the stairs of Geneva College's Center for Urban Theological Studies. I was a little intimidated, but I knew in my heart that God was with me. I felt like this was going to be another turning point in my life.

When I entered, I wasn't sure what to say. I wasn't even sure what I wanted. I asked to speak with a counselor. I knew that would help steer me in the right direction. I met with a counselor, and after a brief introduction and testimony, I let the counselor know that I wasn't sure what God expected of me. I told him how I wanted to be a nurse because I was told I had the gift of healing, but then I mentioned that there was still something missing. My counselor advised me that maybe God wasn't talking about physical healing but rather about spiritual healing. He advised that maybe God's calling was to minister to the spiritually sick people. I was encouraged, so I enrolled in the college. I found out that all my credits from Deliverance Evangelistic Bible Institute and my nursing credits were transferrable. That really put me ahead, and I only needed a few electives. I was astonished at how God worked that out, and I was sure I was on the right course.

I knew I would have to quit my job as a nurse because I could not get the hours off that I needed for school. My classes would take place at night, and I was already working the evening shift. There were no day shifts available. I knew this would hurt our household income, but I talked it over with my husband, and he supported me in my decision. He had faith that we would make it. Remember, sometimes we have to lose in order to gain. Well, after my husband and I made the decision that we could settle for less financially and struggle through me going back to school so I could do the Lord's work, I got a call from an insurance company that was hiring nurses for case management positions. They said they had pulled my resume from their file after they realized they needed to hire one more person. They wanted to offer me the position. They offered me a salary much higher than I had ever made in my life, and the position was for Monday through Friday with weekends and holidays off. I would work from 8:00 a.m. to 4:00 p.m. At first, I thought it was a joke that someone would call out of the blue and offer me a dream job at a time when I really needed it and offer me more money. Once again, I realized God was at work, and I gave Him the glory. I did not remember ever applying for that job. Apparently, I had answered an ad in the paper three months prior and had forgotten about it. Once again, God was on time and worked everything out for my good and His glory. Once my husband and I made the choice to sacrifice and settle for less so that I could go to school, God opened up a window of opportunity and gave me a job with better hours and higher pay, and for once I would not be on my feet all the time. Although I never complained, the long hours on my feet and the pains from lifting many patients in nursing homes and hospitals through the years had started taking its toll on my fifty-five-year-old body. I was getting tired, so this new job came at a good time. The fact that it was a desk job made me extremely happy. God knows just what you need and when to give it to you. I have learned that you never know how God is going to work. You just have to trust Him.

Working full-time and going to school full-time was rough,

but I hung in there by the grace of God and finished with honors, earning a bachelor's degree in Urban Ministry Leadership. I graduated cum laude with a grade point average of 3.7, even though the devil tried to steal it from me in the end with a mix-up about credits owed. Because it was ultimately the college's error, they let me graduate with my class. I was so happy. When I walked up that aisle at graduation I was so happy. I had accomplished something my family had predicted I never would. God was showing me who I could be in Him. In Philippians 4:13, God tells us we can do all things through Christ.

I continue to live a life for Christ. I continue to be a living witness for the Lord. I have learned that we can't live without Him in our lives. Our human nature will fool us into thinking that we are doing all right, but are you living up to God's standards? Better yet, do you know what God's standards are? God's ultimate goal for us is to make us like Christ (1 John 3:1–2). As we become more and more like Him, we discover our true selves, the people we were created to be. In **Romans 8:29 (KJV), Paul says, "For whom He did foreknow, He also did predestinate to be conformed to the image of His Son, that he may be the firstborn among the brethren."** You may ask, "How do you become more like Christ?" First, you must accept Him as your Lord and Savior by confession so that you can be saved. The Word of God also states, **"If thou shalt confess with thy mouth the Lord Jesus, and shall believe in thine heart that God hath raised Him from the dead, thou shall be saved" (Romans 10:9 KJV).** We strive to become more like Him when we read our Bibles and take heed of the Word of God by studying Jesus's life and ministry here on earth through the Gospels (Matthew, Mark, Luke, and John). We must also pray and spend time in prayer. We should fill ourselves with His Spirit, who will guide us into all truth, and we should do God's work in the world.

If you want victory in your life, you have to believe that God is who He says He is and that He is a rewarder of those who diligently seek Him. You must also forgive your offenders and abusers. Forgiveness frees you. Then you must forgive yourself. Get into the Word of God, and let the Holy Spirit guide you and transform your life. Develop a mind like Christ and stop all the negative thinking. In **Romans 12:1–2**, we are reminded not to be like the world, and we should not follow the ways of the world with all of its customs. We are to be different. The only way we can be different is through God's transforming power. We must allow Him to change the way we think.

I heard my pastor Reverend Dr. Allyn Waller of Enon Tabernacle Full Gospel Baptist Church once preach that "we are not human beings on a spiritual journey [but] ... spiritual beings on a human journey." When I first heard him say this, it made me think. When I think about it, I immediately think about Paul's message in **Romans 8**, where he ministers to the people in Rome about living life in the Spirit. In verses 9 through 11, Paul reminds those of us who are saved in Christ that we are no longer controlled by our sinful nature but that we are controlled by the Spirit of God living in us. He further reminds us that those who do not have the Spirit of God living in them are not Christians (the unsaved of the world). With Christ living in us, even though our bodies will die because of sin, our spirits will live because we have been made right with God. The Spirit of God, who raised Jesus from the dead, is the same Spirit living within us. And just as He raised Christ from the dead, He will give life to our mortal bodies by the same Spirit living within us. Paul further advises that that we have no obligation whatsoever to do what our sinful nature urges us to do. If we keep following our fleshly nature, we will perish, but if we turn from our flesh and all its evil deeds through the power of the Holy Spirit, we will live. All who are led by the Spirit of God are children of God. For any Christian struggling with the sins of this world, I recommend you read all of **Romans 8**. It is a good read about living life in the Spirit.

As I reflect on my life, I can testify that when you truly start living a life for Christ through the power of the Holy Spirit, you lose your desire for the sinful things of this life. There are probably many saved people out there with one foot in the world and one foot in the church. Those people are living according to their fleshly nature and haven't truly surrendered their will to God. When you totally surrender your will to God, the secular world has no appeal to you. When you are truly trying to live for God through the blood of Jesus Christ, there is a desire within you to do the right thing.

Salvation saved me. God did not let me die in my sin. Repentance and God's unmerited grace and mercy gave me restoration and my continued sanctification. Today I am a different person. I am becoming the person God designed me to be. I am a living witness for the Most High. I can say without a doubt that God is real and Jesus lives. During most of my early life, I never really felt connected to anything or anyone. I always felt as if I was drifting along by a current of circumstances. I felt like I was just passing through my situations. I would often tell myself that if I just hung in there and didn't give up, the situation would pass. In my ignorance I never realized that was faith. I just called it survival.

The trials of my early childhood and the hardships at my grandparents' house prepared me for the hardships of the streets, and God was with me all along, waiting for me to call on Him. He knew I was walking in ignorance, and He sent His Holy Spirit to protect and guide me. It wasn't until I committed to Christ that my life began to change. I made a lot of mistakes and made some pretty poor choices in my life, but God was faithful to forgive me and cleanse me from all unrighteousness. I will always believe we are all by-products of the choices we make in life. My life has been a testimony to that.

I've had to learn that forgiveness is the key to eternal happiness. I have forgiven all of my abusers. I have let them go, and I do not harbor any resentments. Even though they are not around for me to personally say I forgive them. I have forgiven them in my heart and before God, and I am therefore free. It was hard for me to do this. I remember harboring a hatred for all of them, especially my grandmother, whose love I desired above all. I used to tell people I did not have family. I never felt like family anyway. To me, family was about love, and I never felt love from anyone in my family. Not one person in that large family ever told me they loved me. I carried that pain for a long time in my heart, and it caused me to look for love in all the wrong places. I had to forgive them to free myself. I never knew what it felt like to be loved until God showed me. God's love for me also gave me a love for all people, which is beautiful. My hardships did not harden my heart toward others. As a matter of fact, I used to esteem others over myself, thinking I wasn't good enough. God had to teach me how to love myself, not with a selfish eros love but with an agape love. I had to learn to love who I was in Christ. I had to learn that not everyone saw me the way my family saw me and that their predicted outcome for my life was not part of God's plan for my life. When I fell on my face before God and cried out to Him, He answered. That was the beginning of the restoration.

I no longer live like a victim of my past. I have a peace and a joy that surpasses all understanding. It's a peace and joy that did not come from this world, and the world can't take it away. I have no doubt about my calling from God. At every turning point, He lifted me a little higher.

This book is not so much about me as it is about God and how He has worked in my life (and is still working and sanctifying me) for His purpose and will. This book is my testimony of God's love, His goodness, and His grace, which brought me out of a very painful and desolate place and time in my life. It speaks of God's loving and forgiving nature and how He has blessed my life even though I did nothing to deserve it. God gets the glory, not me. In reading my testimonies, you can see where God was at work in my life. Christian World Ministries teaches that "God is the turning point. The turning around place is in Him! We need God's help! We need God!" It is key that we not only know of the Lord but know Him intimately and be in relationship with Him. It is not an option or an opinion but the truth. We must realize that God is real and that He has thoughts, feelings, power, and pure love. God is pure in thought, intent, and motive. He is for us. He is telling you, "I truly love you. Come to Me." God loves us and knows what's best for us. Anything else is a lie, rejecting Him." I had to learn that being saved was not enough because with salvation there has to be conversion; which is a change in our lives that God produces. There are probably many church members who believe that they are saved, yet they lack the conversion necessary to live truly victorious lives in Christ. There are also people out there who believe that there is a God but go no further than that. There are also people who believe in God, but deny Him the power there of. In other words they don't believe God can and will change their situation. God's Word states that you must not only believe there is a God but also confess with your mouth that Jesus Christ is Lord. Then you are saved. **"If you confess with your mouth that Jesus is Lord and believe in your heart that God raised Him from the**

dead, you will be saved. For it is by believing in your heart that you are made right with God, and it is by confessing with your mouth that you are saved" (Romans 10:9 NLT).

"When you receive Jesus Christ into your heart, His character, and the power of God will bring change into your life. Sometimes it is experienced quickly and at other times it is not as evident" (Christian World Ministries). I find that this is very true for me because I was walking in ignorance as many of us are. I was saved, but there was a period of time between my salvation and my conversion before evidence of my true salvation became apparent. It was my period of trial and error.

Conversion takes place in our hearts through the Spirit of God. When we come into this world we are separated from God because of sin. We become awakened to God through the intervention of His Holy Spirit, which moves us to repentance. When God is alive in us, there is a desire to turn away from sin and our sinful nature. When we acknowledge our sin in the presence of our Holy God through prayer, we realize in His presence how much we fall short of being holy like Him. It is a humbling experience. When we turn to God, we receive His grace and mercy, which gives us the power to turn from our sin and evil ways and to become more like God, moving in His likeness and His ways according to His divine purpose and plan for our lives.

True repentance means turning away from our sinful ways and not desiring to go back. When we are walking in God's truth, we lose our desire for following the ways of the world. He gives us the ability to discern right from wrong. The desire to do the right thing becomes prominent in our lives, and there is an internal conviction when attempting to or when actually doing wrong. If you are following Christ and walking in His truth, that conviction should bring repentance. Once God open's your eyes to the truth about your situation and your life, you can no longer cry ignorance.

That was how I knew God was at work in my life, changing

me for the greater good. I remember how I tried to straddle the fence with one foot in the church and one foot still in the world. I remember going out to a club with some friends. I tried to have a good time and act like I was enjoying myself, but it wasn't the same. I was no longer comfortable with worldly entertainment and the club scene. I knew I had changed. I lost my desire for those things. God was changing my heart. I desired godliness. I was changing, and I liked it. I desired to know more about the things of God, and that desire has brought about great change in my life. I want the people reading this book to know that God looks at who we are in Him, and who we will become, not what we have been. God gives all of us the opportunity to turn to Him if we will. If we renounce life's direction of sin and rebellion and turn to God, He will give us a new direction, a new love, and a new power to change. It is not something we can do for ourselves. It is God's work in us that brings it about. If you have trust in God's power to change your heart and mind, and if you are determined to live each day with Him in control, you will gain the victory over the negative influences and situations in your life.

The first step is accepting Jesus Christ into your heart as your personal Lord and Savior, believing by faith that He is the Son of God and that He died on the cross for our sins, was buried, and rose up on the third day with all power in His hands. It's as simple as that. Then be determined to follow the path of God's truth, not our truth or the world's truth.

It is my hope that anyone reading this book who is facing life's challenges and in need of encouragement will be encouraged by my testimonies and realize that Jesus is alive, God is real, and He is a rewarder of those who diligently seek Him. It is my prayer that you will allow God to deliver you from your struggle and allow Him to transform your life. If you are not living for God and being a living witness to His greatness, then you are not living but merely existing.

You may not have the supernatural experience that I had when I called upon the Lord, and your situation may not be as dire, but I can tell you that God will answer a sincere prayer that is prayed in all humility with a repentant heart. I know my experience with the Holy Spirit was for a purpose, and that purpose is to tell others about the goodness of the Lord in the land of the living.

If you are a saved person but have not undergone conversion, and do not possess a personal relationship with God, you will find yourself struggling with the sins of this world. However, if you turn away from sin, seek God's help, repent, and ask God's forgiveness, He will undoubtedly forgive you. His unmerited grace and mercy will allow you to start over, and you will begin to walk in His truth.

The thing we need to remember is that God loves us and that it is not His desire that anyone of us should perish. He desires that we have eternal life. That is why He sent Jesus, His only begotten Son, to be a substitute for our sins and to save us from eternal destruction. Just because we are saved does not mean we are infallible. If we are not praying, not reading our Bible, and not developing a personal relationship with God by spending time alone with Him so He can minister to us, then we will fall into the ways of the world and become easy prey for the devil. Satan is real (for those of you who may not believe it), and he is roaming around like a lion, seeing how many he can destroy **(1 Peter 5:8)**. Satan is our adversary. He is conniving and deceitful above all. He is also a defeated foe. It is written in God's Word. The Christian, the one who is striving to live for God, is Satan's target, and if you are not in a relationship with God, you have made Satan's job easier.

If you are not saved, it is my hope that you will be encouraged by my testimonies and make the decision to accept Christ into your heart by faith and confession. Let God work in you. Trust in

Him so that you can achieve victory over your struggle or trials. Then you will come to know God's truth and start to walk in it. If you are living a defeated life and have lost all hope, try Jesus. He is our hope.

1Peter 1:13–25 (NLT) is a call to holy living for those of us who are saved. The apostle Peter reminds us:

> "Think clearly and exercise self-control. Look forward to the gracious salvation that will come to you when Jesus is revealed to the world. So you must live as God's obedient children. Don't slip back into your old ways of living to satisfy your own desires. You didn't know any better then. But now you must be holy in everything you do, just as God who chose you is holy. For the scripture says you must be holy because I am holy. And remember the heavenly Father to whom you pray has no favorites. He will judge or reward you according to what you do. So you must live in reverent fear of Him during your time as foreigners in the land. For you know that God paid a ransom to save you from the empty life you inherited from your ancestors. And the ransom paid was not mere gold or silver. It was the precious blood of Christ, the sinless, spotless, Lamb of God. God chose Him as your ransom long before the world began, but He has now revealed Him to you in these last days. Through Christ you have come to trust in God. And you have placed your faith and hope in God because He raised Christ from the dead and gave Him great glory. You were cleansed from your sins when you obeyed the Truth, so now you must show sincere love to each other as

brothers and sisters. Love each other deeply with all your heart. For you have been born again, but to a life that will quickly end. Your new life will last forever because it comes from the eternal, living Word of God".

This book is a praise report to glorify God. I cannot and will not forget that He saved me, strengthened me, delivered me from the pit of hell, and then put my feet on solid ground. He continues to sanctify me for His divine purpose and will for my life. He is showing me who I am in Him and all that I can be. My grandmother thought that I would "amount to nothing" because of my parents failings, but God took what was bad and turned it into something good. I want people to know that there is a Savior who can and will deliver them from whatever trials and persecutions they may face. Whatever legacy your family or the world has spoken into your life, you don't have to live it out because, **"you belong to God, my dear children. You have already won a victory over those people, because the Spirit who lives in you is greater than the spirit who lives in the world" (1 John 4:4 NLT).** You see, you belonged to God first, and He made us with a divine purpose and will for our lives. We cannot fail if we follow Him and live according to His statues, which He laid out for us in His Word. God's Word is alive and it speaks to the very essence of our souls.

I sometimes reflect on the time in January 1999 when my husband and I survived that fire. We lost everything we owned except the clothes on our backs. I remember we prayed and gave it all to God. We did not pray about the fact that we had lost everything. We prayed for others who had also lost a lot and for our friend who had lost her life in that fire. We let God know that our hope was in Him. He had already given us more than we ever deserved or could hope for, and we knew that we had been living for Him and striving to live according to His will and purpose for our lives. The day after the fire was put out, my husband and the insurance adjuster walked through the remnants of our home. The place was totaled. The most beautiful part was when my husband brought home the only thing that truly survived the fire—our Bible. It was found sitting on the floor in the center of what had been our den. It was singed on the outside and wet from the fireman's hoses, but the inside was intact. The pages were damp but not soaked. When I saw that, I cried because I knew God was there in the midst of it all and He wanted us to know it. If we had gone to bed, we would probably not be here today, but it was not part of God's plan that we should perish in that fire. He was true to His Word to never leave us or forsake us. We had no worries that God would see us through this, and He did. In **Matthews 24:25**, God said that heaven and earth would disappear but His Word would never disappear. And in Hebrews 4:12, He said His Word is alive and powerful.

It is so important that we not just know the Word of God but also believe it. And if we believe it, the evidence of that belief should show in the way we live. I started out in life not knowing much about this wonderful and great sovereign God, the Creator of heaven and earth, and because of that lack of knowledge, I suffered the consequences of the wrong choices I made in life. I was walking in ignorance of Him even though I came from a family where many were saved, but like me, they did not truly know the Lord. Low self-esteem, abuse (verbal, emotional, and physical), dysfunction, and rejection had become my norm. Not many people knew how I was feeling. I suffered in silence. Family members judged that silence as a negative thing. They thought I was sneaky. I knew I couldn't win their hearts, so I kept quiet. But

God knew my heart, and when He started opening my eyes to His goodness, His grace, and His forgiveness, I made a decision to live for Him and Him only. I have never regretted it.

To quote the all-inspiring words of Maya Angelou, "You did what you knew how to do, and when you knew better, you did better." I once heard it said that "your past is your school of experience, let your past mistakes point you to God". I did. I sought Him with my whole heart, and He delivered me from all my fears.

—ᘉ—

Take a moment and reflect back over your life. Think about your journey. What is it that you have overcome? What situations or hardships have you survived? All of us have been delivered from someone, someplace, or something. You've survived it. Who do you give credit to for your survival? There are many who say, "I did all by myself. Nobody helped me. I pulled myself up by my bootstraps". Well, I am here to tell you how wrong you are. The only reason you may have a measure of success in your life is because of God, and Jesus paved the way for it by shedding His blood. God has been working in our lives to get us to trust in Him. Many of you don't even realize it. Through your trials He sustained you. He deserves all of the praise, the glory, and the honor. He has allowed some things to happen in our lives to show us that we can do nothing without Him and to point us in the direction of the one and only true God. That's not to say God causes bad things to happen to us. We mostly suffer from the wrong or poor choices we make when we leave God out of our lives. God did not promise that we would not go through trials and struggles. The struggles we face in life actually help make us stronger. As a matter of fact, struggles will pursue you and try to trip you up as you move further into God's presence. The more you strive to follow God, the more the devil tries to distract you and may even attack you, but God has promised in His Word that whatever we go through, He will be with us.

> **But now o Jacob listen to the Lord who created you, O Israel the one who formed you says, "Do not be afraid, for I have ransomed you. I have called you by name you are mine. When you go through deep waters, I will be with you. When you go through the rivers of difficulty you will not drown. When you walk through the fire of oppression, you will not be burned up; the flames will not consume you. For I am the Lord you God, the Holy One of Israel, your Savior. (Isaiah 43:1–3 NLT).**

It is my hope that as you reflect on your own turning points, you will realize that God has been there all along, using your situations and conditions to turn you toward Him.

The following are a few key steps to achieving the victory in your life:

1. The very first step is to receive Jesus Christ into your heart by faith (if you haven't already). You can say this prayer, and God will hear you if you really mean it. **"Dear heavenly Father, I have been going down the wrong road, and I want to make a U-turn toward You. I believe that Jesus is the Son of God. I believe that Jesus died and rose from the grave so that I may have eternal life with You. Please forgive my sins and come into my life. Fill me with Your love and the power of the Holy Spirit. Write my name in the Lamb's Book of Life. In Jesus's name. Amen."**

2.   Believe that God is who He says He is.

3.   You must have forgiveness in your heart for all of your offenders/abusers. Forgiveness frees you from the negative hold their actions may have over your life.

4.   Forgive yourself. One of the hardest things for us to do is to forgive ourselves. When God opens our spiritual eyes to our sin, we are embarrassed. We spend far too much time feeling guilty long after God has forgiven us. It's a trick of the devil so that you won't move forward in Christ. Accept God's grace, and let God start moving you in the direction of His purpose and plan for your life.

5.   Get into God's Word, and let the Holy Spirit lead you and transform your life. If you don't own a Bible, get one. It is important that you know and understand the Word of God.

6.   Stop all negative thinking. Develop the mind of Christ. Think on those things that reflect love, joy, peace, patience, kindness, goodness, faithfulness, gentleness, and self-control **(Galatians 5:22)**.

7.   Become Christ-minded. Ask yourself, "What would Jesus do.?" I once read that "having the mind of Christ involves abandoning our own will and ego, putting others needs first, and humbling ourselves to serve even to the point of great personal sacrifice." That's exactly what Jesus Christ, the King of glory, did for us (christianhomechurch.com).

References

Holy Bible, Spirit-Filled Life, Thomas Nelson, Inc., 1982.

Holy Bible, Life Application Study Bible, Tyndale second edition.

Holy Bible, Broadman & Holdman, 1996.

Christian Word Ministries, Prayer Book, 428 Southland Drive, Lexington, KY.

James Robison, The Holy Spirit and Restoration, Spirit-Filled Life Bible, Thomas Nelson, Inc., 1982.

Printed in the United States
By Bookmasters